The Catholic Church:
A Brief History

The Catholic Church:
A Brief History

by
Alfred Lapple

translated by
Peter Heinegg

Paulist Press
New York/Mahwah

Maps by Kevin Novak, C.S.P.

Originally published 1982 as *Kirchengeschichte Impulse zur Kurskorrektur* by Don Bosco Verlag, München.

Library of Congress
Catalog Card Number: 84-62152

ISBN: 0-8091-9567-4

Published by Paulist Press
997 Macarthur Boulevard
Mahwah, N.J. 07430

Printed and bound in the United States of America

Contents

1

Beginnings: The First Century

The history of the Christian Church is inextricably bound up with the name of the man who was the protagonist in the drama of its origin: Jesus of Nazareth. Jesus and his work were later considered so important that he became the pivotal point in the reckoning of time. People spoke, and they still do, of B.C. and A.D.

Despite the fact that he came to grief on the cross before his fortieth year, Jesus' message remained alive, first of all in Palestine, and very quickly spread to important centers of the Roman Empire (Ephesus, Athens, Corinth, Rome). "And in Antioch the disciples were for the first time called Christians" (Acts 11:26). All over the Mediterranean basin men and women were increasingly won over to the Christian community.

In the century of its birth the Church found itself confronting three basic themes of its existence.

Ever since 63 B.C. Palestine, Jesus' homeland and the native soil of the Christian Church, had been incorporated into the Roman Empire. This political situation was one of the reasons why the apostles and their co-workers, with Paul at their head, traveled west on their proselytizing journeys, toward the Mediterranean region.

Rome's worldwide empire, with its unity, organization, good roads, safe sea routes, and almost universally understood languages (Greek and Latin), provided an ideal territory for the Christian missions and the spread of the Church.

The geographical shift and international expansion westward added breadth and depth to the Christian community's sense of itself. That community was no longer a little sect limited to Palestine. It presented itself as a universal Church made up of Jews and Gentiles, as the religious homeland of all languages, peoples, and cultures.

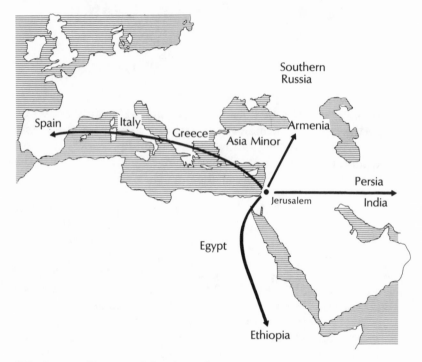

Missionary Routes of the Apostles

Writing Down Jesus' Message

Historical research has concluded that we do not have a single document written by Jesus himself. Nor do we have so much as one eyewitness account of Jesus composed before his crucifixion.

Starting around the middle of the first century A.D. certain authors were led, for very different reasons, to compose pieces that would be gathered together in the following century under the title "New Testament" (in contrast to the Old Testament), as the book of the Christian Church. Along with Pastoral Letters (especially those written by Paul) there were four Gospels, intended for various audiences, the Acts of the Apostles, and a prophetic book, the secret Revelation of John.

These writings appeared so late because many Christians had at first looked for Jesus to return soon. After this expectation collapsed, one factor that prompted the creation of the New Testament was surely the widely felt desire to have an authentic, eyewitness report about Jesus. But there were other motives for writing down these texts, such as debates within the community, the desire to eliminate the scandal of the cross, and liturgical needs, as well as the encounter with contemporary Jewish and Greek intellectual trends.

The writings of the New Testament provide us with a unique view of the complexities of the early Christian *kerygma* (proclamation), as well as of the growth of the first Christian communities, their sense of identity and the differences between them.

Early Tensions and Problems

Church history confirms the law of world history: the transition from any "founder" to the first generation after his death decides whether a message or a community will survive.

We are informed that at the dawn of Church history the believers were "of one heart and soul" (Acts 4:32). At the same time newly founded Christian communities such as Corinth were the scene of "dissensions" (1 Cor 1:10), petty jealousies, and competition for status (1 Cor 11:18). The growth in the number of Christians led to an expansion of the organization, to the founding of new positions, and a division of labor—a process that caused some friction. "Now in these days when the disciples were increasing in number, the Hellenists murmured against the Hebrews because their widows were neglected in the daily distribution" (Acts 6:1). Because of this deacons were appointed to care for the poor.

But on a deeper level there were vehement discussions and

differences of opinion among the apostles and their co-workers over the concept of the apostolic mission. Peter represented the Jewish-Christian view while Paul spoke for the Gentile Christians. Should Jesus' message and offer of salvation, as Peter first argued, continue to be limited to the Jews—and hence should Jewish-Christian communities be the only ones established? Or, as Paul, "the apostle of the Gentiles," passionately maintained, was Jesus' salvation meant for all men and women, and should all nations become disciples of the Lord (Mt 28:19)?

Paul tells us quite frankly how hard the struggles and clashes were. He does not hesitate to report that "when Cephas (Peter) came to Antioch I opposed him to his face, because he stood condemned [for claiming that Jesus' message was for Jews alone and that therefore Gentiles had to undergo circumcision]. . . . I saw that they were not straightforward about the truth of the Gospel" (Gal 2:11, 14).

At the "council of the apostles" there was open dispute, not over personal prestige, but exclusively over the Lord's cause. After arguing with and against one another—but also after praying together for the spirit of truth—the "dissension" (Acts 15:2) was resolved by declaring that the community of Jesus Christ unites the Jews and Gentiles who have been called to it. It is home to all nations and languages, a fellowship in the Lord embracing the manifold variety of peoples, languages, cultures, ways of thinking, and modes of faith.

First Conflicts with Political Authority

As early as the first century conflicts arose between the Church and the secular political power of the Roman Empire and its emperors. Actually this confrontation might not have occurred, for the Roman policy toward religion up till then had been liberal and tolerant. Rome had previously had serious trouble only with observant Jews and, as a result, had granted them special protection to practice their religion.

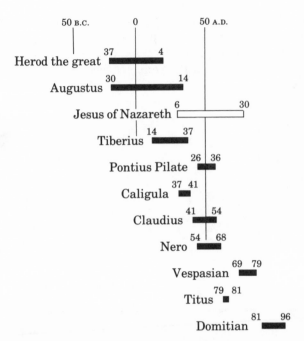

Jesus and the Reigns of First Century Rulers

So we may ask whether it was merely a series of misunderstandings, of malicious calumnies and imputations, that led Rome to move for the first time against the Christians and the heads of their communities, the apostles and their co-workers. In the Church's first century the Roman legal system evidently had not yet developed any arguments and fixed rules to justify the unleashing of a persecution against the Christians.

But it grew increasingly clear that Christians could not take part in the Roman imperial cult—the mandatory veneration of the emperor as a god. Sooner or later, then, there would have to be conflicts between Christians and the religious laws and decrees of the Roman Empire. In the first century some Christians were martyred, such as Peter and Paul in the reign of Nero, or exiled, as John was banished to the island of Patmos. And there were waves of local persecution.

All these signs pointed to an intensifying persecution, which Christian communities experienced in the following two centuries.

Key Dates in Church History

ca. 30 A.D.	Jesus of Nazareth dies on the cross in Jerusalem under Pontius Pilate
50–120	The books of the New Testament are written down
ca. 64–67	Martyrdom of the apostles Peter and Paul (under Nero)

Chronology

CHURCH HISTORY	SECULAR HISTORY
	63 B.C. Pompey brings Palestine under the Roman yoke
	44 B.C. Julius Caesar assassinated in Rome
	37–4 B.C. King Herod I
	31 B.C.–14 A.D. Emperor Augustus
ca. 7 B.C. Birth of Jesus	**14–37** Reign of Tiberius
	26–36 Pontius Pilate, Roman procurator in Palestine
ca. 30 Jesus' death on the cross	
ca. 34 Saul's conversion on the road to Damascus	
40–61 Missionary journeys of Paul the apostle	**41–51** Reign of Claudius
50–120 Composition of the books of the New Testament	**50–116** Cornelius Tacitus, Roman historian
	54–68 Reign of Nero
64–67 Martyrdom of the apostles Peter and Paul in Rome	**64** Fire of Rome
67–76 Linus, first successor of the apostle Peter in Rome	**67–73** Jewish War
	68 Destruction of the Jewish Monastery of the Essenes* at Qumran* on the Dead Sea
	70 Destruction of Jerusalem by Titus, son of Emperor Vespasian (69–79)
76–88 Anacletus, second successor of Peter in Rome	
	81–96 Reign of Domitian
90–99 Clement, bishop of Rome	

*Words or phrases marked by an asterisk are explained in the Glossary at the end of the book.

2

An Era of Trials and Tribulation: The Second and Third Centuries

The work and message of many important personalities in world history have had little ongoing effect on later times because their personal activity was not followed by convinced adherents and propagandists. The reason why Jesus' work and message found their way into the mainstream of world history (insofar as this can be studied and documented by scholarly methods) is that after Christianity's first century came a two hundred year period of crisis and testing which, though very stormy, was of positive importance in many respects.

Explosive Expansion

The rapid expansion and dispersion of the Christian communities throughout the Roman Empire, clearly evident by the end of the second century, was a remarkable phenomenon. While older Christian communities solidified, especially in Palestine and Asia Minor, increasingly large concentrations of Christians appeared in southern and central Italy (including Sicily and eventually Sardinia as well) and on the North African coast around Carthage.

In the third century an almost totally Christian territory was taking shape in southern Spain. In southern France, in the districts along the Rhine and Moselle Rivers, and in England rapidly growing Christian centers sprang up, most of them headed by bishops. Historians have demonstrated that this fast-moving expansion can be traced back, on the one hand, to the well constructed highways of the Roman Empire, which practically beckoned to the messengers bringing news of the Christian faith, while on the other hand a large number of Christians settled in the garrison towns scattered all over Europe (far from imperial Rome) in order to escape the fierce persecutions in Italy, Greece, or Asia Minor.

Christian Centers at the Start of the Fourth Century

After careful reckoning the following figures may be cited for the growth of Christendom:

> *1st century:* ½ million Christians
> *2nd century:* 2 million Christians
> *3rd century:* 5 million Christians

If we estimate the total population of the Roman Empire around the beginning of the fourth century at roughly fifty million, then by the midpoint of this century, when the Church won its freedom thanks to Emperor Constantine, the number of Christians in the entire Empire can be set at ten million or so.

Development of the Church's Structure

Even in the Pauline communities tensions arose between the Church's leadership (nowadays we would say the institutional Church) and charismatic individuals and certain powerful undercurrents. Paul stated emphatically that "God is not a God of confusion but of peace" (1 Cor 14:32), and he defended his own teaching authority with hardly surpassable intensity: "If . . . an angel from heaven should preach to you a gospel contrary to that which we preached to you, let him be accursed" (Gal 1:8).

As early as the end of the first Christian century it proved necessary to point to "sound doctrine" (1 Tim 1:10; 2 Tim 4:3), to "the truth that has been entrusted to you by the Holy Spirit" (2 Tim 1:14) as opposed to erroneous interpretations. At the same time Christians had to have their attention called to the Church's urgent, if unpleasant, task of giving directions and making decisions: "Proclaim the message, press it home on all occasions" (2 Tim 4:2). It was not just the growth of the Christian communities that called for a separation of offices and functions. It was above all theological questions and challenges from within the Church that both created the need for, and hastened the development of, a responsible body to govern the Church. Drawing upon the basic inspirations and commissions given by Jesus himself to Peter, to the apostles as a group, to the wider circle of the disciples, and to all the people of God, the way of life of the Christian communities and dioceses grew in various forms while maintaining an organic identity.

As this took place, a fundamental importance became attached to the union of those communities and dioceses with the Roman church and to its bishop, who was esteemed as Peter's successor. The Roman church was acknowledged as the "head of the alliance of love" (Ignatius of Antioch*). Irenaeus of Lyon* said of Rome: "Every other church must concur with this church on account of its special pre-eminence." Cyprian of Carthage* speaks of the necessary solidarity in belief with Rome: "To be in communion with the bishop of Rome is to be in communion with the Catholic Church."

Definition of the New Testament Canon

Even in the Gospel of Luke we find a note that "many have undertaken" (Lk 1:1) to write about Jesus. So as to distinguish his work clearly from these novelistic treatments of Jesus, Luke explains his intention, "having followed all things closely for some time past, to write an orderly account . . ." (Lk 1:3). Later, as the biographies of Jesus kept proliferating, a collection of the four Gospels according to Matthew, Mark, Luke, and John, which was binding upon the whole Church, was produced around 150 A.D.

But when Marcion (around 140) put together a highly arbitrary selection of "Holy Scripture," the leaders of the Church found themselves compelled to specify the writings that were to be regarded as the obligatory canon (rule) of the New Testament. The only texts to be accepted into this canon were those that had been used in the official liturgy of the Christian communities. The so-called "hidden" writings (the apocrypha), employed by sectarians and secret groups hostile to the Church, were denied official recognition.

Doubtless the most important document illustrating the process of compilation and the extent of the New Testament canon toward the end of the second century is the Muratori

Fragment, named after Ludovico Antonio Muratori, who discovered it in the Ambrosian Library in Milan and first published it in 1740.

Christian Teaching Exposed to Misunderstanding and Distortions

Growing up as it did in the Roman Empire, with a host of competing philosophies, religions, and myths of redemption, the Christian faith sooner or later had to engage in radical conflict with these currents of thought (which included, in the political sphere, the worship of emperors).

One such powerful current—which had a Christian air about it, but for that very reason presented a serious danger—was gnosticism (and related world-views). The Gnostics cherished the hope of achieving salvation through "knowledge" (*gnosis** in Greek) and contempt for the "evil" material world. This school (and under the heading of gnosticism belong docetism,* neo-Platonism,* and Manichaeanism), with its highly pious and ascetic behavior, stood in the front line of the assault against the Christian idea of creation, against the incarnation of the Son of God, and against redemption through Jesus' death and resurrection.

In addition the Christian Church had to defend its faith in the triune God against Jewish monotheism while at the same time opposing the pagan misinterpretation of belief in the Trinity as tritheism (the worship of three gods).

Within the Church a particularly explosive issue was the baptism of heretics: whether Christians who had been baptized by an apostate priest or bishop had to be rebaptized when they came back to the Church. Behind the discussions over baptizing heretics looms a dark shadow: the record of the Christian communities was not one of unimpeded growth. A large number of lay people, priests, and bishops apostatized in North Africa, for example. And even in Rome around the middle of the third century vigorous efforts at founding a counter-Church were launched under the anti-popes Hippolytus and Novatian.

The Church and Roman Imperial Theology

Ever since the assassination of Julius Caesar on March 15, 44 B.C. the custom had arisen of a senatorial decree announcing the deification of the Roman emperor and conferring on him the honors due a god. Emperor Domitian (81–96 A.D.) proclaimed himself "Lord (*kýrios*) and God" (cf. Jn 20:28). So long as Trajan's rescript from 112 A.D. was in force, individual Christians could be charged and taken to court only by private accusers, and so the flame of persecution did not burst into a conflagration.

After the year 200, however, as the Roman Empire was increasingly threatened, especially on its northeastern flank, by the Germanic tribes, and people were blaming the Empire's troubles on the decay of Roman religion and its cultic sacrifices, some of the emperors looked to save the Empire by placating the gods and reviving the state religion, while attacking the Christians. A decisive battle with Christianity became inevitable. The Christian religion was declared harmful to the Roman Empire and forbidden. But could the emperors expect to win such a battle with the Church after the number of Christians in the Empire had already passed five million?

To view the early Christian period as bathed in an enviable romantic glow of undisturbed inner harmony is historically untenable. The Christian community, despite all the resistance it met, did enjoy a considerable growth in numbers and geographical expansion. Along with this, however, went a steady supply of problems, very few of which involved overcoming political pressure from the Roman Empire.

As far back as the second and third centuries the Church had to learn how to deal with controversial trends of the day by presenting Jesus' message in a fresh, up-to-date, but integral form for the needs of a changing world. Even the ancient model of the "little flock" had to be developed creatively. Practical ways of living and decision-making had to be devised for the growing communities and dioceses. These first organizational and theological blueprints had a profound influence on the later shape of the Church, which moved not eastward, but toward the western Roman Empire, and which to this day bears a European stamp.

Key Dates in Church History

ca. 180	The Muratori Fragment (New Testament canon)
ca. 220–260	Attempts at founding a counter-Church in Rome
from 200 onward	Systematic persecution of Christians (interrupted by periods of peace): assault on the Church's organization (200–249), systematic mass persecutions (249–311)

Chronology

CHURCH HISTORY	SECULAR HISTORY
60–200 Persecution of Christians as individual persons	
	98–117 Reign of Trajan
	112 Trajan's rescript (provided legal basis for proceeding against Christians)
	117–138 Emperor Hadrian
140 Age of the Christian apologists	
ca. 160 Death of Marcion*	**161–180** Reign of Marcus Aurelius
ca. 180 Death of Montanus*	
ca. 180 Muratori Fragment	
	193–211 Reign of Septimius Severus
ca. 180 Schools for catechumens in Alexandria, Caesarea, and Antioch Theological debates within the Church (docetism, gnosticism, Manichaeanism, Monarachianism, adoptionism)	
196 Victor I, bishop of Rome (189–199), settles the dispute over the feast of Easter Increased respect accorded the pre-eminence of the Roman church and its bishop (the letter of Clement, Victor I, Stephen I, Irenaeus of Lyon, Cyprian of Carthage*)	

CHURCH HISTORY	SECULAR HISTORY
	212 Emperor Caracalla (211– 217) grants Roman citizenship to all free inhabitants of the Empire
Anti-popes Hippolytus (217– 235) and Novatian (251– 258)	
202–249 Systematic persecution of Christians	
	216–276 Mani, founder of Manichaeanism*
ca. 220 Death of Tertullian*	
	249–251 Reign of Decius
250–251 First general persecution of Christians under Decius	
	253–260 Reign of Valerian
254 Death of Origen*	
255–257 Dispute over the baptism of heretics	
ca. 270 Beginnings of eremetical life in Egypt (St. Anthony, d. 356)	
	284–305 Reign of Diocletian
	293 Restructuring of the Roman Empire by Diocletian
303–311 Persecution of Christians begun by Diocletian	

3

The Church Amid Political Upheavals:
The Fourth and Fifth Centuries

As a community of faith the Church is admittedly not of this world, but it lives and works there. It is exposed to the vicissitudes of political power—the special favors and the persecutions. For almost three hundred years the authorities of the Roman Empire maintained a critical, often hostile distance from Christians. Around the beginning of the fourth century, however, this relationship underwent a radical shift that would have a far-reaching impact not just on the future of Christianity but on the religious and political shape of the West.

Constantinian Christianity

Up until this point the Christian faith had been given the official political stamp of *religio illicita* (forbidden religion). Christians were persecuted because they were believed to be enemies of the state. But from the middle of the third century B.C. onward, despite anti-Christian propaganda, the number of Christians increased considerably, especially in the eastern provinces and most notably among civil servants and soldiers in the legions. Even though a reversal of the Empire's policy toward Christianity seemed scarcely imaginable, sooner or later it had to come. After Emperor Galerius had set the stage by issuing an edict of tolerance in 311, Constantine (d. 337) effected a definitive change in Rome's treatment of religion.

The Edict of Milan (313), which was an agreement between Constantine and his co-emperor Licinius, and especially the

Edict of Theodosius I (dated February 28, 380) declared Christianity to be the religion of all the peoples of the Roman Empire. The Christian religion thereby took over the political function of safeguarding the Empire that had formerly been exercised by the pagan religion of imperial Rome. Empire and Church entered a coalition built upon a common interest, simultaneously strengthening the unity of faith and the Church as well as the unity and future security of the political system. The Empire went into partnership with the Church, as the Church did with the Empire, in order to insure their chances of survival. This would lead to far reaching consequences for both partners.

The emperor now thought of himself as the protector of the Church. It was his political concern to watch over the faith, to promote its expansion, to defend Church unity, and to ward off, convert, or condemn the enemies of the faith (heretics). It was the emperor who interfered in religious controversies racking the Church, and he convened the First Council of Nicaea (325) as an imperial council under his own auspices. In turn the Church supported and deepened the secular power's awareness of a religious responsibility and mission through the anointing and crowning of the emperor. By stressing and paying special respect to his sacred office and "divine right" the Church gave him honor and prestige in the eyes of all the people.

The coalition of Church and Empire, Pope and emperor, religious force and political power ushered in some splendid achievements—as the history of the West clearly demonstrates—but it also unleashed tragic events and bitter discords. Again and again each side fought against the other for freedom and autonomy. They had violent arguments, trying to shake off the other's all too possessive embrace. The Church had to struggle for its freedom and self-determination against encroachments by the emperor (and various other sovereigns). And not infrequently secular princes offered resistance to the Church (Popes and bishops). The Constantinian coalition of Empire and Church was a very quarrelsome association. Too often the only thing keeping it together was pressure from outside enemies.

On the subject of this great turning point in Church-state relations, Walter Dirks observes: "The mistake of choosing the

Constantinian system led, via the conversion of the Germanic tribes, into the imposing dead-end street that we call the Middle Ages." Even though "Constantinian Christianity" underwent many changes over the centuries (along with the shifting political regimes), it has continued, at least in Europe, to function as a modus vivendi and form of cooperation between Church and state until the present.

Concern for Creedal Unity at the Imperial Councils

The new freedom granted the Church by the Edict of Milan (313) did *not* inaugurate a springtime of faith or consolidate the unity of the Church. On the contrary, once Christians no longer needed to worry about their lives being in danger, they had time to busy themselves more actively with the meaning and interpretation of the truths of their faith. The days of external political peace became for the Church a time of grave religious dissent and schism.

At the center of these controversies stood the mystery of the incarnation. Beliefs that had been accepted as a matter of course were now subjected to urgent questioning, especially by philosophically trained Christian converts. How were Christians to understand (and explain to others) what the New Testament says about Jesus? Jesus maintains that "the Father is greater than I" (Jn 14:28). Concerning his knowledge of the end-time he says, "But of that day or that hour no one knows, not even the angels in heaven, nor the Son, but only the Father" (Mk 13:32). What was one to make of Jesus' cry of abandonment as he hung on the cross, "My God, my God, why hast thou forsaken me?" (Mk 15:34; Mt 27:46 = Ps 22:2).

Was Jesus a mere human being? Is he really the Son of God made man? How was the union of true man and true God in Jesus, the Christ, to be understood? Did the incarnate Son of God have only one will—a divine one? Wave after wave of questions came pouring in upon the Christian world, receiving contradictory answers and shaking to its foundations the unity of belief and of the Church. The Christian community of faith, having escaped political catastrophe, was now threatening its own life through self-laceration.

It was a sign of the times that in the face of these internal Christian disputes Emperor Constantine felt obliged, as protector of the Church, to look after the unity of the faith. Speaking of the convocation of the First Ecumenical Council at Nicaea (325), Eusebius of Caesarea, the emperor's court biographer, writes: "Constantine bade the council assemble like an army of God. With respectful letters he requested the bishops to come quickly. He also directed the state postal service to transport the council fathers or to provide them with draft animals. As the meeting place for the council he designated a very well-suited town, Nicaea in Bithynia."

In the fourth and fifth centuries the following imperial councils were convened:

TIME	PLACE	MAIN THEME
325	Nicaea (I)	The divinity of Christ (identity of essence between God the Father and God the Son): as opposed to the teaching of Arius*
381	Constantinople (I)	The Divinity of the Holy Spirit: as opposed to the teaching of Macedonius*
431	Ephesus	The divine motherhood of Mary: as opposed to the teaching of Nestorius*
451	Chalcedon	Two natures (divine and human) in one (divine) person of Christ ("hypostatic union")

Looking back at these conciliar discussions and pronouncements about Jesus, we can see that the participants were not content with the letter of the Christian message as delivered by the New Testament. Those very texts had stirred up conflicting opinions, because Christians who spoke Greek and had Greek intellectual habits also had a natural tendency to ask probing critical questions. They wanted to know things exactly and to peer (out of curiosity, pious or otherwise) into the depths of the incarnate Son of God.

But this process of critical illumination and rational support of the Church's faith in Christ could take place only through the concepts and modes of thought made available by Greek philosophy. When the Church confronted misinterpretations of Christian faith, such as the one advanced by Arius ("Jesus Christ is a creature of God. Therefore there was a time when he did not exist"), the Church found itself compelled, when it met at the councils, to speak about Jesus, the Christ, with extreme precision and clear conceptual language. The theologians and council fathers, with their Greek habits of thought, experienced a kind of pious intoxication as they poured out their beloved technical terms, hoping to find in them security for the Christian faith.

But Hilary of Poitiers* must have realized the dangers posed by this highly conceptualized theology. He was deeply concerned and warned against "doing what is not permitted, climbing to precipitous heights, saying the ineffable, venturing recklessly into forbidden places." A tendency had emerged leading from the wisdom of the cross to a science of the cross, from a theology of contemplation and adoration to a theology of analysis and critical examination. The mystery of faith became the object of scholarly research, to be explained with precise systematic terminology.

Yet there was another decisive element affecting both this intellectualization of faith in Christ and the catechetical process of spreading it: the great "doctors of the Church" in both the East and the West, for the most part, were also bishops. So their theological work was not done in abstract, theoretical isolation, but took its inspiration and tone from pastoral care, from the needs, questions, objections, and religious problems of the various Christian communities.

Tribal Migrations—Spread of Arianism

While the councils of the fourth and fifth centuries struggled to maintain the integrity of the Christian faith, an altogether different sort of event paved the way for Arianism, which had already been rejected as heresy: the migration of the barbarian tribes that began around 375. Jerome, the erudite translator of the Bible into Latin, expressed his horror at the religious consequences of the migration when he said, "The entire world awoke and groaned to discover that it had become Arian."

The Visigoths, Ostrogoths, and Vandals were Arians. The Arian bishop Wulfila, who translated the Bible into his compatriots' mother tongue around 350, became famous as the "apostle of the Goths." Wherever the Visigoths, Ostrogoths, and Vandals established their kingdoms, Arian territorial churches sprang up. And while Theodoric, king of the Ostrogoths (471–526), was tolerant toward the "Catholic" religion, in North Africa the Vandals practically destroyed the "Catholic" church, with its three hundred or so dioceses.

This was the first schism to strike the European Christian world. Orthodox Christians, who clung to the faith of the councils, were in the minority, and they had reason to be anxious about their chances for survival. Whereas the Church, which treasured the conciliar faith, had joined together with the now collapsing Roman Empire ("Constantinian Christianity"), the condemned teachings of Arius were backed by the power of the new Germanic kingdoms and spread all over Europe and North Africa.

The question was: When the Roman Empire collapsed, would the Church also break down, since it had such close ties with that political force? Would the Arian faith, even though it had been condemned at the ecumenical (general) councils of the fourth and fifth centuries, be swept along in the van of the victorious Germanic tribes and win out over the "Catholic" faith of the councils?

From the standpoint of the secular historian, one has to say that the Germanic kingdoms proved to be short-lived and grad-

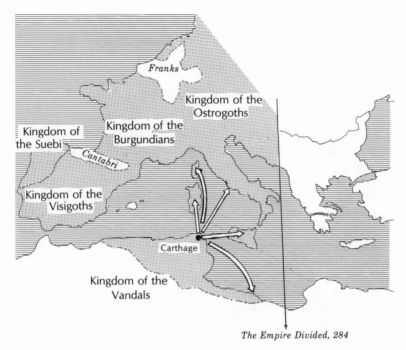

The Empire Divided, 284

The Arian Germanic Kingdoms

ually collapsed themselves, and this spelled the end of Arianism's brief heyday. Some relevant dates here are:

> 533   Downfall of the North African Kingdom of the Vandals
>
> 553   Downfall of the Ostrogoth Kingdom
>
> 711   Downfall of the Visigoth Kingdom (in Spain)

Arianism (together with the translation of the Bible into Gothic and the development of Gothic as a liturgical language) undoubtedly helped the Visigoths, Ostrogoths, and Vandals to prevent the loss of their ethnic identity. Only after they abandoned the solid ground of their own language did their religious and ethnic identity disintegrate. Their ways of life and belief were Romanized by the adoption of Western political and "Catholic" forms.

Political Upheavals and Increased Authority for the Bishop of Rome

As head of the community associated with the apostles Peter and Paul, the bishop of Rome understood his role as Peter's successor to mean that he was responsible for the unity and purity of the Christian faith. He was widely respected and appealed to as the decisive authority by bishops and synods in Asia Minor, Spain, and North Africa.

As early as the initial period of the Age of Constantine this preeminence was given still greater emphasis. In 378 Emperor Gratian (375–378) specifically established the jurisdiction of the bishop of Rome as legally binding. But the Church of Rome was intent on asserting its autonomy, as we can gather from a decree by the Roman synod convened by Pope Damsus I (366–384). In what is surely a reference to the law enacted only a few years before by Emperor Gratian, the synod declared: "The holy Roman Church did not receive its preeminence over the other churches through the decisions of any council (and still less from imperial law), but through the word of our Lord and Savior, 'You are Peter, and on this rock I will build my church' (Mt 16:18)."

Actually the political situation brought the bishop of Rome a considerable increase of authority, especially in the case of the highly effective Leo I (440–461). After the imperial residence had been transferred from Milan to Ravenna, Rome felt, even more than in the recent past, like a nonentity in the world of power politics, helplessly exposed to the oncoming Ostrogoths. The troops of the Western Roman Empire could not stop the advance of the barbarian tribes. At this fateful point Leo I* proved to be the defender and rescuer of Rome and Western culture by managing to turn Attila away from Rome in 455. In this turbulent period, when the patterns of Church life were breaking down in Gaul, the provinces on the Rhine, and even northern

Italy, the bishop of Rome was the only reason for hope in the future of Christian faith.

The experiences of the tribal migrations showed that only the Roman church—together with its bishop—was built on a solid foundation. The sun of God's grace seemed to shine on Rome alone. As he gained political prestige the bishop of Rome also extended his authority to decide questions of faith and other internal Church issues. This is evident from the enthusiastic cries of the council fathers at Chalcedon, "That is the faith of the fathers and the apostles. Peter has spoken through Leo."

The bishop of Rome emerged from the tumultuous period of tribal migrations and the short-lived Germanic kingdoms. Rome, to quote Pope Leo I, "the see of St. Peter, became the head of the world."

Key Dates in Church History

313	Edict of Milan (Constantinian Christianity)
325	Council of Nicaea (I)
375	Beginning of the tribal migrations (spread of Arianism)
391	Christianity becomes the state religion of the Empire
451	Council of Chalcedon

Chronology

CHURCH HISTORY	SECULAR HISTORY
	311 Edict of Toleration of Emperor Galerius
	312 Battle at the Milvian Bridge (near Rome)
313 Edict of Milan	
313–383 Wulfila (Gothic translation of the Bible—Codex Argenteus—ca. 350)	
325 Council of Nicaea (I) Eastern Doctors of the Church:	**330** Consecration of the new imperial city Constantinople (New Rome)
Athanasius (295–373)	
Basil the Great (331–379)	
Gregory Nazianzen (330–390)	
John Chrysostom (354–407)	
	361–363 Emperor Julian the Apostate
	375 Beginning of the tribal migrations
381 Council of Constantinople (I) Western Doctors of the Church:	
Ambrose (340–397)	**391** Christianity becomes the state religion of the Empire, thanks to Emperor Theodosius (379–395)
Augustine (354–430)	
Jerome (340–420)	
Gregory the Great (d. 604)	
	395 Division of the Roman Empire into Eastern and Western Empires
	410 Rome sacked by the Visigoths (Alaric)
431 Council of Ephesus	
440–461 Leo I, the Great	
451 Council of Chalcedon	

CHURCH HISTORY	SECULAR HISTORY
	451 Battle at Châlons; Attila (d. 453) defeated
	455 Sack of Rome by the Vandals (Genseric)
	476 End of the Western Roman Empire
	486 Clovis' victory over Syagrius (last Roman governor of Gaul)

4

New Ventures, New Orientations
for the Church: From the Sixth
to the Tenth Centuries

When the Western Roman Empire collapsed toward the end of the fifth century (476), many theologians and bishops were afraid that the Church, which for some two hundred years had thrown in its lot with the political power of the Empire, would be swept away by the same catastrophe.

It is an historical fact that with the downfall of the short-lived kingdoms of the Ostrogoths, the Visigoths, and the Vandals, the predominance of Arianism was broken once and for all. What theological condemnations at various councils and even direct political action failed to achieve took place because the barbarian kingdoms passed so quickly from the scene. The precarious condition of both the state and the Church strengthened both the political position of the Eastern Roman Emperor and the ecclesiastical position of the patriarch of Constantinople, the imperial city of Byzantium.

But it was obvious that the bishop of Rome (we recall Pope Leo I*) could substantially increase his authority—in the West, at any rate—*because* of this time of troubles. And given the need to get a clear orientation for the present as well as to make plans for the future, this meant that a power struggle was inevitable. From the beginning of the sixth century onward, the question was: How would the patterns of conflict among the three sovereigns—the Pope of Rome, the patriarch of Constantinople, and the emperor of Byzantium—actually resolve themselves? Did the bishop of Rome, like his predecessors, have no other choice but to place himself under the protection of the emperor? Would the Pope and patriarch end up competing for the emperor's favor?

Looking ahead into the Church's future, we might well feel the tension as we follow the historical process that would be played out by those three authority figures. It would profoundly affect the peoples of both the East and the West. The years to come would be marked by the ruthless calculations of power politics and the sometimes brutal jostling for position within the Church.

A Baptism—A Turning Point

It was an entirely personal decision when Clovis, king of the Franks, whose Catholic wife Clotilda came from Burgundy, had himself baptized by Bishop Remigius at Christmas, 496 in Rheims. Neither the bishop nor the king could have known that this baptism was to become a turning point in history.

But a bare hundred years later Gregory of Tours (538–594) seems to have sensed the world-historical importance of the event when, in his *History of the Franks,* he calls Clovis "a new Constantine." This was a conscious attempt to make a connection, after the downfall of the Western Empire, with the tradition and Church-state commitments of that Empire's earlier days. Constantine's legacy and mission were still in force. They had not been transferred to the emperor residing in Constantinople. Only Clovis, king of the Franks, should be regarded as the legitimate successor to and executor of Constantine's legacy.

One may take a skeptical view of the goings-on in the chancelleries of the Frankish kings and their bishops. We may dismiss ideas like Gregory's as a clever bit of "political theology" or clerical propaganda, or as barbarian presumption or Germanic arrogance. But the fact remains that north of the Alps as early as the sixth century the Church was laying claim to a share of the government, and the state was pledging loyalty to the Church.

Into the contest of Pope, patriarch, and emperor a fourth

player had now made his way, uninvited but impossible to ignore: the king of the Franks and his successors from various ruling houses.

The proud opening lines of the *Lex Salica,* the customary law code promulgated by Clovis (d. 511), suggest that the "Age of Constantine" has had a second flowering, that a new alliance between throne and altar offers great hopes for the future:

Long live Christ, who loves the Franks!
May he guard their kingdom
and fill their princes
with the light of his grace.
May he protect their army
and defend the faith!

Protector of the Church—More Than a Title?

Without discussing the political events of the time or the successful work of Christian missionaries in continental Europe, we can still get an overview of what the privileged position of "new Constantine" meant for the Frankish kings.

Around two hundred and fifty years after the baptism of Clovis, Pippin the Younger (741–768) was honored by Pope Stephen II (752–757) with the title "Patricius Romanorum," protector and defender of the Roman church and the Catholic faith (754). The granting of this title, whose immediate occasion was the threat from the Lombards, sent out a very clear and irritating signal to the emperor of Byzantium and the patriarch of Constantinople. They were indignant, and not simply because the Pope had bestowed this distinction on a "barbarian." Now the outside world could see that the link between the Pope of Rome and the head of the Eastern Roman Empire (once himself the "Patricius Romanorum") had been severed.

A new Rome-France axis now became a political reality, and for many centuries to come it would prove its value. The papacy's turning away from the East—on the political level, to begin with—was now complete. Many events thought of as archetypal moments in European history are rooted in the alliance between Church and Empire, Pope and emperor; for instance there was the coronation of Charlemagne in Rome on Christmas Day, 800, the Italian campaigns of the German emperors, the coronation of the Holy Roman emperors, the Crusades, or even the intervention of Charles V against Martin Luther at the Diet of Worms in 1521. This association between the Church and the Empire was also the reason for the longevity, for the climactic moments and agonizing episodes, of that more than one thousand year period called the Age of Constantine.

A letter from Charlemagne written in 796 to Pope Leo III (795–816) gives us a clear picture of this relationship of mutual aid and support—which sometimes led to bitter struggles for supremacy. "It is our task," writes Charlemagne, "with God's help to defend the holy Church of Christ everywhere with the force of arms against attacks from without by the heathens, and the ravages of the infidels, and to strengthen the knowledge of the Catholic faith within the Church. Your task, most holy Father, is to help our armies by lifting up your arms to God, as Moses did, so that through your intercession and God's command the Christian people may always and everywhere win the victory over the enemies of his holy name, and the name of the Lord Jesus Christ may be glorified throughout the world."

The Christian West Enveloped by Islam

The homeland of Islam and its founder Muhammad (570–631) was in Arabia, and it seemed to pose no danger to Europe and its development. But the breakneck speed of its expansion soon gave Europeans a rude awakening. And Islam would have a notable influence on Europe's historical and intellectual development.

Starting out from the Arabian peninsula, Islam surged across the whole southern coast of the Mediterranean. From the East it thrust into the southeastern flank of Europe, while in the West, once it reached Gibraltar, it got a firm foothold in Spain and for a time even managed to penetrate into France. Europe had begun to recover from the distress and confusion of

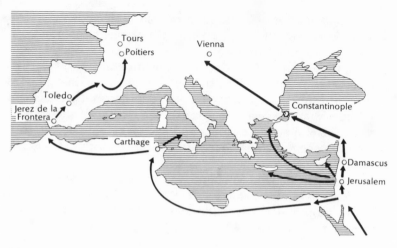

The Pincer Movement of Islam

the tribal migrations, and the political and religious situation had stabilized somewhat, just when it was caught in Islam's pincer movement. Flourishing Christian communities were strangled and destroyed, like those in North Africa where not long before Cyprian of Carthage* and Augustine of Hippo* had worked. Equally important was the fact that the ties between the West and Eastern Christianity, already strained by the papacy's favoring the Frankish kings, were almost entirely cut off by the spread of Islam. The missionaries, too, found their access to the Far East closed off. Only by taking the irksome land route across Russia and Siberia in the thirteenth and fourteenth centuries did Franciscans and Dominicans succeed in pressing through to China, then under the power of the Mongols, where they preached the Gospel and organized a branch of the Church with an archbishopric in Beijing.

Church and Empire were forced to transfer their activities "inward." We tend to take for granted the historical reality called "the Christian Middle Ages," with its atmosphere of lofty spirituality and artistic power, but all that was, among other things, the result of the concentration of energy in a Europe that had been constricted and, indeed, encircled by Islam. The intelligentsia never left home. The strongest forces in politics, the arts, philosophy, and theology had to face a host of competitors within the narrow bounds of Europe. One might compare Europe to a sort of boiler under too much pressure which would not be relieved until the end of the fifteenth century, mainly through the discovery of the New World and of the sea routes to the Far East.

Up to this point we have described the external framework of early medieval Europe. Now we have to consider its inner evolution, as it prepared to adopt a fresh perspective in Church-state relations even while being hard pressed by Islam.

Benedict, Father of the West

In 529, when Benedict founded a monastic community on Monte Cassino, north of Naples, he was hoping to establish a place for recollection and worship, clearly marked off from the rest of the world, amidst a hectic and unsettled age. This monastery was to be a refuge, and its password was "Ora et labora" (Pray and work).

The Benedictines were bound by vow to observe *stabilitas loci* (to live permanently in one place). The Christian was supposed to find his home in God and his security among his brethren. But ironically the Order of St. Benedict first made a great name for itself in Church history when its basic character, as envisioned by its founder, underwent some notable modifications.

Shortly after Benedict of Nursia died, his ideas were given a radical rethinking by Pope Gregory I, the Great (590–604). This Pope was confronted by the urgent problems of evangelism among the Germanic peoples. As he saw it, the crucial pre-conditions for effective missionary work were theological education, team spirit, and fidelity to the Church. So from Gregory's time onward a continual stream of Christian missionaries flowed out from Benedictine monasteries, and Benedict himself received the title "Father of the West."

The achievements of the Benedictine monks can be sum-
marized by three symbols: the cross (they were messengers of
the Christian faith), the book (pioneers and preservers of Western culture), and the plow (promoters of civilization and new
settlements). According to the English historian Edward Gib-
bon, "A single Benedictine monastery may have done more for
the cause of knowledge than Oxford and Cambridge combined."

The Second Wave of Missionary Activity

Across many parts of Europe Roman Christianity had been
overwhelmed or totally destroyed by the advance of the Arians.
On the European mainland population shifts and colonization
had occurred, and so a second campaign had to be launched to
preach the Christian faith.

It was no accident that the missionaries now came from the
countries and islands that were not threatened by the Arianism
of the tribal migrations. In England, Ireland, and Scotland Roman Christianity had been able to flourish almost undisturbed,
and for this reason they could serve as bases for the evangelization of their Germanic tribal brothers.

This kinship was a stroke of good fortune. It helped to create a rapport with the Germanic tribes, it simplified the process
of learning their customs, and above all it made it easier to
frame the Christian message in ways appropriate to the audi-
ence. The peculiar character of the Germanic tribes, their
strong sense of clan and family, their whole way of life, all left
a clear imprint on their image of Christ and their understanding of the Church and its sacraments.

The theological concepts and evangelizing methods of the
individual missionaries were quite different—corresponding to
their different home monasteries, Irish, Scottish, or Anglo-
Saxon. Some of these missionaries, for all their hard work and
dedication, were very self-willed, and they resisted being incorporated into any overarching Church organization—as Boniface, the apostle of Germany, learned only too well when he
tried to organize the German church and strengthen its bonds
with Rome.

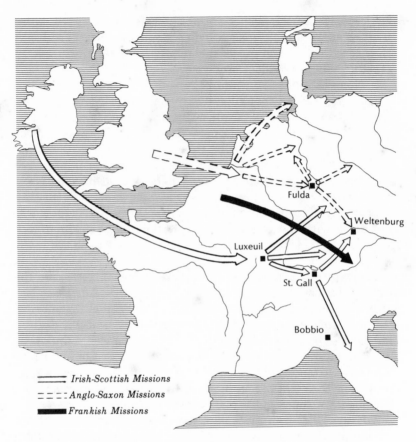

Missionaries of the Sixth to Ninth Centuries

Mass Baptisms and Armed Evangelization

It is astonishing how quickly the Germanic tribes were won over to Christianity. But we should beware of crediting the "conversion" of these peoples to a personal decision on their part for the faith. They were illiterate and had been given only a brief period of religious instruction. Their notion of the relationship between a lord and his followers required that the religious beliefs of the local prince or duke be adopted by his subjects. Hence the Christian missionaries were first directed to the leaders of the clans and tribes, without whose permission they could not preach the Gospel in any given territory, or even erect a chapel or outdoor cross.

No evangelization could begin until the tribal prince had been converted. In speaking of the "converted" Germanic peoples, therefore, we must realize that their faith was syncretistic, for it still contained remnants of pagan belief that survived and flourished for a very long time. The well-known Reformation dictum, *Cuius regio, eius et religio* (the ruler of any area decides what his subjects' religion will be) has deep roots in Germanic tribal consciousness, and was applied as early as the fifth century. Whenever there was opposition to Christianity it was put down with the sword, in utter defiance of "freedom of conscience." Stubborn individuals were soon forced to adjust to the new order.

A typical—and essential—feature of the conversion of the Germanic peoples was the right of "proprietary churches." Not only did the lord of a region prescribe the faith of his subjects (thereby making them serfs both spiritually and physically), but he also had the exclusive right to build churches and monasteries on his land. Along with this went the right of patronage, that is, to attend to the building and upkeep of the church, as well as the right to nominate the pastors of his churches and the abbots of the monasteries he had founded.

Every Christian sovereign was thus a "little Constantine" who undoubtedly was concerned with maintaining and promoting the Church and Christian faith, but who sometimes put his interests ahead of the Church's rights.

Key Dates in Church History

496	Baptism of the Frankish king Clovis
529	Founding of the Benedictine monastery of Monte Cassino
754	Pope Stephen II grants Pippin the title "Patricius Romanorum"
910	Founding of the monastery of Cluny

Chronology

CHURCH HISTORY	SECULAR HISTORY
	476 Downfall of the Western Roman Empire (Emperor Romulus Augustulus deposed by Odoacer)
496 Baptism of Clovis	
529 Founding of Monte Cassino by Benedict of Nursia (d. 547)	
	532 Downfall of the Burgundian kingdom
	533 Downfall of the Vandal kingdom
553 Second Council of Constantinople	**553** Downfall of the Ostrogoth kingdom
	570 Birth of Muhammad in Medina (d. 632)
590–604 Pope Gregory I, the Great	
680–681 Third Council of Constantinople	
730 onward Iconoclastic Controversy	

CHURCH HISTORY	SECULAR HISTORY
	754 Pope Stephen II (752–757) anoints Pippin king and names him "Patricius Romanorum"
	756 The Peace of Pavia ("Donation of Pippin")
	768–814 Emperor Charles the Great (Charlemagne)
787 Second Council of Nicaea	
794 Frankish General Council in Frankfurt	
	800 Coronation of Charlemagne in Rome
858–867 Pope Nicholas I	
858 Tension between Rome and Photius, the patriach of Constantinople	
860 onward mission to the Slavs led by Cyril (d. 868) and Methodius (d. 885)	
869–70 Fourth Council of Constantinople	
910 Founding of the Monastery of Cluny	

5

A Powerful Church and Missed Opportunities for Reform: The Eleventh to Fourteenth Centuries

The period from the eleventh up to and including the fourteenth centuries is called the Middle Ages because it lies between antiquity (which ends, a large number of historians maintain, after the age of Charlemagne) and modern times. Geographically, the "Middle Ages" are increasingly extended to cover Eastern Europe as well, since it was the time when Christianity entered the world of both the Germanic-Neo-Latin *and* the Slavic peoples.

In any case the Middle Ages were anything but a homogeneous period. They provided a discontinuous setting in which the Church played out a bold, complex, exciting, but ultimately unsuccessful adventure. The path followed by the Church during the Middle Ages has been characterized as an "impressive dead-end" (Walter Dirks). We can speak of the "Christian" Middle Ages only with many reservations. A singular wave of unrest swept over the people of God then: they felt a growing sense of disappointment, which led to increasingly loud and urgent calls for a credible Church.

Positions of Leadership

Around the year 1000 Christendom was shaken by a violent end-of-the-world fever. It was believed that after a time when the devil had been "chained for a thousand years" (Rev 20:2) the last phase of human history would occur. Only a little while remained, and then the great day of judgment would come. Once this feverish expectation had faded and been forgotten, Christendom began to settle down on an ever more solid and permanent basis in this world. Of course, there were at that time no national states in the modern sense, but among the peoples of the West a sort of division of labor had developed: intellectual leadership came from the many philosophical and theological centers in France or, more precisely, the land between the Seine and the Rhine. This was the source of a continual stream of intellectual, cultural, and theological impulses. Spiritual leadership came from Italy where the Pope resided, the successor to St. Peter. Political leadership came from Germany and its emperors, as we see in the expression, "Holy Roman Empire of the German Nation."

An Age of Contrasts

The period between the eleventh and the fourteenth centuries was rich in contradictions. It witnessed a thoroughgoing intellectual revolution in art, philosophy, theology, modes of worship and piety.

In art the Romanesque style gave way to Gothic. The great open space created by Romanesque architecture for the liturgical community was now divided up into many little chapels, where the individual could engage in solitary prayer. The Romanesque image of Christ the King was replaced by the Gothic image of the crucified Man of Sorrows. Medieval philosophy and theology received profound new stimuli from contact with the work of Aristotle, who was just becoming known in the West.

The great theologians and mystics and many other people were disturbed by the inadequacies of a Church that badly needed reform. Theologians were building their mighty intellectual systems, like Gothic cathedrals. At the same time popular piety was flourishing—and so did the remnants of paganism within it. People spoke of God and grace, but they often tried to assure their own salvation and eternal bliss through crude, old-fashioned magic. The distinct outlines of a developing individualism loomed on the horizon.

In the Middle Ages contradictions jostled hard against one another, even in the same person—"untrammeled enjoyment of life and gruesome pleasure in terror and death, humble contrition and ruthless egoism, risqué courtly dances and the grim, bloody processions of the Flagellants, godly cathedrals soaring titanically to the sunlit heavens—and down in the narrow streets hate, mistrust, shameful superstition and the dark obsession with witchcraft" (Anton L. Mayer).

Spreading the Gospel with the Sword

Beginning with the Carolingian Age Christian missionaries knew they could count on the protection of the emperor or sovereign. The upshot of this was that the tribes and peoples which converted to Christianity largely forfeited their political autonomy and were incorporated into the power structure of the protecting sovereign. Thus the mission to the Wends (1147), led by Henry the Lion, duke of Saxony and Bavaria, which sought to convert the peoples living between the Elbe, the Saale, and the Oder, turned into a campaign of extermination against the Slavs. The leaders spoke of God, but they meant politics. They preached the Kingdom of God, but at the same time they were intent on land and power.

The Slavic peoples would suffer grievously from the "Christian mission" because they happened to live in places of political interest to both the Frankish and Byzantine rulers who were trying to extend their power into Slavic lands. Along with its missionaries the Church was caught up in the political rivalries between East and West. When territorial sovereignty was at stake, neither side hesitated to engage in sordid intrigues, to hire informers, to kidnap and murder. The political violence marking the Slavic mission seriously impeded relations between Rome and the Christian East. And so it should come as no surprise that among the newly converted tribes and people there were outbreaks of both anti-Frankish (anti-Western) and anti-Byzantine violence.

The Crusades, too, were proclaimed as wars of religion, in keeping with their pious slogan, *"Deus lo vult"* (God wills it).

What was originally a campaign launched by the Church in the name of faith degenerated as early as the capture of Jerusalem (1099) into a shocking, orgiastic bloodbath, as the account by William of Tyre (died ca. 1185) bears witness. Later the Crusades became naked struggles for power, as when Byzantium was ruled, from 1204 to 1261, by the Latin kingdom of Constantinople.

Religious dream and political reality now had practically nothing in common. Turkish Muslims watched the scandalous spectacle of Western Christians fighting Eastern Christians— and not over religion, but for political power.

———— Land route

- - - - - - Sea routes

The Crusades

The Papacy: Powerful and Powerless

The Middle Ages were constantly punctuated by conflicts between the papacy and the Empire. There was a "Dark Age" in the tenth century during which, thanks to the German emperors, the Church escaped from the crossfire of competing factions among the Roman nobility by the nomination of six German bishops to the papacy—though of course this exposed the Popes to the equally strong influence of the Empire.

A short time later, when the German Emperor Henry IV was forced to go to Canossa (1077) to have the ban of excommunication lifted, Pope Gregory VII could show the Christian West who had the upper hand in both spiritual and worldly matters. But then came the great schisms of 1159–1177 and 1378–1417, when a perplexed Christendom was sometimes faced with the spectacle of a "villainous duo of Popes becoming a damnable trio." This was the papacy's darkest and most powerless moment.

Popes Innocent III (1198–1216) and Boniface VIII (1294–1303) pressed their claims to universal power in bitter earnest. In speaking of Boniface VIII we can scarcely avoid terms like papal absolutism and imperialism, or even clerical fascism. "His passionate desire to make the papacy great," writes Joseph Bernhart, "was a personal desire to become powerful by means of the papacy. He did not serve the office, but made it serve his own purposes."

Yet the power of the Popes was in an unsettled condition then, and it could quickly turn to impotence, as demonstrated by the political dependency of the seven French Popes who lived in Avignon during the "Babylonian Captivity" from 1309 till 1377. Many Western observers considered the Avignon Popes "bishops of the French court" and despised them for it.

Toward the end of the Middle Ages papal credibility and authority were very badly shaken. The popular outcry for a general council grew louder and louder. It seemed to be the only hope to save the Church and assure its future. Increasing skepticism about the papacy fueled expectations of the council, which was supposed to achieve—all by itself—a bold and long overdue reform of the Church "in head and members."

The Split Between East and West

An event that had been in the making for centuries came to a logical but scandalous conclusion on July 16, 1054. On that day Cardinal Humbert, acting on behalf of Pope Leo IX, delivered a bull of excommunication against the patriarch of Constantinople, Michael Cerularius. The bull was placed on the altar of Hagia Sophia in Constantinople (which, like every altar, symbolized redemption, peace, and Christian unity), and thereby became legally binding.

Many sharply contested differences in theology and sacramental practice had led to this estrangement. In addition, Eastern and Western bishops had wrangled for centuries over rank and order of preference. Another decisive factor was the conflict between the political forces backing the Pope of Rome on the one hand and the patriarch of Constantinople on the other, clashing head-on during the mission to the Slavs and the Crusades.

Differing views about theology and liturgy helped to create hostile parties within the Church. Clerical narrow-mindedness and petty monastic jealousies resulted in a process of ugly, mean-spirited self-laceration. Ultimately, all sorts of animosities, theological, political, and no doubt psychological, caused and consolidated the break between Rome and Constantinople, between the Western Church and the Eastern Church.

A sort of ecclesiastical iron curtain came slamming down, and only in the twentieth century (1965) was the bull of excommunication lifted by the Second Vatican Council, and a dialogue of faith and love begun, to explore the possibilities for a future reunion.

Scholastics and Mystics

The spiritual and intellectual breadth and complexity of the Middle Ages become evident when we look at the tension between Scholasticism* and mysticism*. Few people realize what a revolutionary impact the rediscovery of Aristotle* had on medieval higher education. The great Greek philosopher was evidently considered a dangerous influence because in 1210 a Parisian provincial council banned his writings, a prohibition that was repeated in 1215, 1245, and again in 1263. The well-known Franciscan theologian Bonaventure went so far as to talk about "whoring with Aristotelian reason."

It was no less a figure than the Dominican theologian Thomas Aquinas* who read the works of Aristotle, despite their being on the Index, and made extensive use of them in his own work. In so doing he instigated a radically new departure in theology, a revolution with scarcely foreseeable consequences. Up until then Christian thinkers like Bonaventure had looked upon theology as *sapientia*, as knowledge of the faith and salvation, designed to lead to a state of existential involvement, to absorption in contemplative prayer, to the imitation of Christ.

By contrast, Thomas Aquinas took Aristotle's ideas on knowledge and made them his point of departure. He understood theology in the scientific sense of formal doctrine, *scientia*. In his view theology as a science had to be based on rational argumentation and be subject to an autonomous scientific theory of knowledge. With their keen intelligence and their propensity for system-building the Scholastic philosophers and theologians left behind them some tremendous achievements.

But when it adopted the Aristotelian method and strove to create a comprehensive system, theology was also capable of degenerating into absurd logic-chopping exercises, as in the proverbial question raised by late Scholasticism of how many angels could fit on the head of a pin. It was no accident that such hair-splitting disputations, which heated the brain but chilled the heart, gave rise to a sense of apathy and inner emptiness. Into this scene of religious desiccation came the mystics of the fourteenth century, pointing the way to the experience of blissful consolation. It was the heart, they argued, that knows God, not the understanding. This introspective, Augustinian piety offered hope and encouragement to many people who had grown disgusted with the insubstantial fare of later Scholasticism.

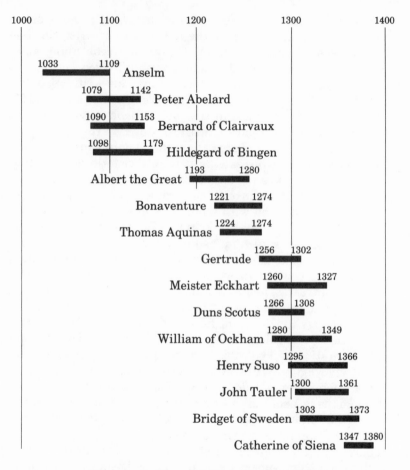

Demands for a Believable Church

From the twelfth century on the forces of religious unrest became increasingly more powerful as they took shape in a broad spectrum of groups and movements (Cathars,* Albigensians,* Waldensians,* etc.). But practically every challenge issued to the Church, every passionate appeal for change, was charged with heresy, condemned, and "eliminated" in massive, tragic purges. It is an oversimplification and a real injustice to the many heretics who had the truth on their side and the courage to defy death, when efforts are made to dismiss heretics as alienated outsiders who claimed to be wiser than the Church. Rather, as Heinz Flügel says, "The dogmas of the Church were written down with the blood of heretics."

Heretics were accused of being "enemies of public order" in the Church and the Empire. But in each case we must scrupulously examine whether the heresy was really a distortion of the Church's teaching or whether the heretics were not calling attention, in their obstinate and self-punishing way, to abuses in the Church, to wrong or inadequate interpretations of the faith. In any event, the tragedy of the persecution and burning at the stake of countless heretics is inexcusable.

In discussing heretics Augustine once made a bold and profoundly honest remark: "Don't think that heresies could arise through the work of a few beggarly little souls. All the heretics were great men." What was the common thrust of most of the late medieval heretical movements? Almost without exception it was *not* disobedience to the Church, but a concern and responsibility for the Church. Given the tension they felt between their affirmation of Jesus and their need to criticize the Church as it actually was, the heretics could no longer keep quiet. The time of silence had passed. The time for them to speak out, when they *had* to speak out, had begun.

Almost all the movements charged with heresy invoked the Bible. At the same time they directed their most violent attacks at a Church that had become rich and powerful, that played by the rules of this world instead of living in the spirit of Jesus the poor man. It is not hard to understand why, in the midst of the Albigensian crisis and in the face of their obligatory daily readings from Holy Scripture, a Synod of Toulouse decreed in 1229: "Apart from the psalter and the breviary lay people are not to own any book of Holy Scripture. And they are not to have copies of these in the vernacular. In addition we forbid the laity to have books of the Old or New Testament in their possession, unless they should wish, out of devotion, to have their own psalter or breviary or Book of Hours of the Holy Virgin. But we strictly forbid them from having such books in the vernacular."

Toward the end of the Middle Ages there was no more stifling the demand for a Church renewed in the spirit of Jesus and made believable once again. This demand, to be sure, died many times over in the bonfires of the Inquisition. By the end of the "Christian" Middle Ages hopes for a reformed Church based on poverty, fidelity to the Bible, and the imitation of Christ remained unfulfilled. Often enough it was the persecuted, defeated heretics who proved to be creative and innovative pioneers of the Church's future.

Key Dates in Church History

1054	Separation of the Eastern from the Western Church
1077	The Canossa Controversy
1096–1270	Crusades
1122	Concordat of Worms
1231	Establishment of the Papal Inquisition
1309–1376	"Babylonian Captivity" of the Popes in Avignon

Chronology

CHURCH HISTORY	SECULAR HISTORY
910 Founding of the monastery of Cluny by William of Aquitaine	
	919–1024 Saxon domination of Germany and the Holy Roman Empire
	955 Victory of Otto I over the Hungarians at Lechfeld
German Popes: Gregory V (996–999) Clement II (1046–1047)	

CHURCH HISTORY	SECULAR HISTORY
Damasus II (1048) Leo IX (1049–1054) Victor II (1055–1057) Stephen IX (1057–1058) **1001** Founding of the archbishoprics of Gniezno (Poland) and Esztergom (Hungary)	
	1024–1125 Salic or Frankish emperors **1042** King Edward the Confessor in England
1054 Schism of Eastern Church	**1056–1106** Emperor Frederick IV in Germany
1059 Regulations concerning papal elections (laid down by Pope Nicholas II, 1058– 1061) **1073–1085** Pope Gregory VII **1075** Prohibition of lay investiture	**1066** Norman invasion of England
	1076 Jerusalem captured by the Turks **1076** (January 24) Deposition of Pope Gregory VII by the Synod of Worms
1077 (January 25–27) Emperor Henry IV does penance at Canossa	**1079–1142** Peter Abelard
1096–1270 Crusades **1090–1153** Bernard of Clairvaux **1098–1179** Hildegard of Bingen **1122** "Concordat" of Worms **1130–1202** Joachim of Floris	
	1138–1244 Rule of the Hohenstaufen in Germany

CHURCH HISTORY	SECULAR HISTORY
1140 Cathars become active, especially in southern France	
	1147 Crusade against the Wends, led by Henry the Lion (1130–1195) **1150** Founding of the University of Paris **1152–1190** Emperor Frederick I, Barbarossa

1159–1177 Papal schism
1176 Waldenians became active
1182–1226 Francis of Assisi
1184 Synod of Verona: introduction of the episcopal Inquisition
Theologians:
  Albert the Great (1193–1280)
  Bonaventure (1221–1274)
  Thomas Aquinas (1225–1274)
  Duns Scotus (1266–1308)
1198–1216 Pope Innocent III	

	1204–1261 Latin Empire of Constantinople **1215** Magna Carta
1209–1229 Albigensian Wars waged by Simon de Montfort and Louis VIII	
	1222 Founding of the University of Padua **1224** Founding of the University of Naples
1224 Introduction of the Inquisition into Lombardy (by agreement between Pope Gregory IX and	

CHURCH HISTORY	SECULAR HISTORY
Emperor Frederick II), extended to the entire Empire in 1232 **1231** Establishment of the papal Inquisition **1264** Introduction of the Feast of Corpus Christi New Religious Orders: Carthusians (1084) Cistercians (1098) Premonstratensians (1126) Carmelites (1156) Franciscans (1210 or 1223) Dominicans (1216) Hermits of St. Augustine (1256) **1294–1303** Pope Boniface VIII **1309–1276** Captivity of the Popes in Avignon **1320–1384** John Wycliffe **1337–1380** Catherine of Siena Mystics: Eckhart (d. 1327) Tauler (d. 1361) Suso (d. 1366) Ruysbroeck (d. 1381) **1378–1417** Papal schism	**1268** Conrad, the last Hohenstaufen, executed in Naples by Charles of Anjou **1291** Three oldest Swiss cantons join together **1337** Hundred Years War begins between England and France **1348** Bubonic plague strikes Europe **1348** Founding of the University of Prague **1365** Founding of the University of Vienna **1386** Founding of the University of Heidelberg **1388** Founding of the University of Cologne

6

A Renewed Church—Or a New One?
The Fifteenth and Sixteenth Centuries

In discussing European intellectual history during the fourteenth and fifteenth centuries the Dutch historian Jan Huizinga called that period "the waning of the Middle Ages." This oft-quoted phrase can easily be misunderstood to mean that after the richly creative High Middle Ages the two following centuries were marked by a pattern of intellectual, cultural, and religious exhaustion and atrophy.

As Europe drew nearer to the dividing line that would separate the Middle Ages from the modern period the signs of a great coming upheaval became increasingly clear. Dissatisfaction with both the Church and the Empire grew more intense, but beyond that there were indications pointing to radical change in the world of the mind, to a new vision of religion and society.

Resignation or Hope?

From the twelfth century on the demand for a believable Church became increasingly radical and vehement, especially among the Cathars, Albigensians, and Waldensians. It was a passionate cry that could no longer be silenced. The hopes of believing Christians for a Church renewed in the spirit of Christ and his Gospel could be put down by the rack and bonfires of the Inquisition, but only case by case. When local flare-ups gave way to a smoldering, spreading conflagration, there was little to be done.

As an indication of the way intellectual, geographical, political, and ecclesiastical horizons broadened in the fifteenth and sixteenth centuries, we may mention five leading figures:

> Johann Gutenberg (ca. 1400–1468)
> Girolamo Savonarola (1439–1498)
> Christopher Columbus (1451–1506)
> Niccolò Machiavelli (1469–1527)
> Nicholas Copernicus (1473–1543)

These men lived in the same era, but their life's work was astonishingly varied. Each of them represents a uniquely different aspect of the modern effort to comprehend and master the world. A new understanding of God, the Church, man, and the universe was in the making.

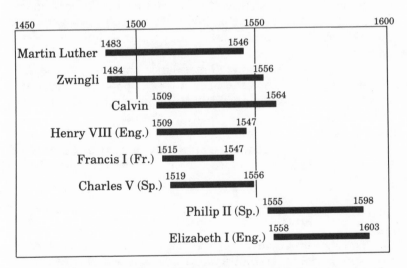

The Church had grown rich and powerful, but anyone who looked past the surface could see its fragility and internal contradictions. The papacy played the part of a self-assured dominant power, but the long years of conflict between Popes and anti-popes, each periodically excommunicating the other's followers, and not least of all the captivity of the Popes in Avignon

(1309–1377), lowered their prestige, particularly in Germany, and cast their supranational authority into doubt.

Large sections of Christendom held fast to distorted marginal truths of the faith: veneration of saints and relics, accumulation of indulgences, going on pilgrimages. Many Christians were driven (and tormented) by an extravagant, egocentric idea of salvation and a highly quantified ethic of earning merit. Thus in the Castle Church of Wittenberg around the year 1517 (just when Martin Luther was making public his ninety-five theses against the traffic in indulgences), it was possible for a believer, by reciting prayers and devoutly contemplating the elector's relic collection, to accumulate 1,900,000 years worth of indulgences. "One can only call this a pious orgy with numbers, raising precautions over the afterlife to unimaginable heights," said historian Martin Brecht. Wittenberg had a dangerously attractive competitor in the collegiate church of St. Moritz in Halle, because in 1520 the rich store of relics there produced more than thirty-nine million years of indulgences.

The marble facades of Renaissance churches soared impressively upward, but the back alleys of popular piety were narrow and gloomy. Belief in the devil and witches, not to mention anxiety over judgment day and the eternal fires of hell, turned the good news preached by Jesus into an ominous message of terror. What remained of the Gospel that had promised to make people happy and free, to bring them consolation and peace?

Motives Behind the Reformation

Thousands of bishops, priests, and religious were aware of the Church's loss of credibility, of the desperate problems it had, and of the miserable state of popular religion. They suffered, prayed, and did penance for the sake of Church reform. But why did this smoldering situation burst into flame in a John Wycliffe, a Jan Hus, a Girolamo Savonarola, a Martin Luther, a Huldreich Zwingli, or a John Calvin, to name but a few? Evidently they had a particular kind of sensibility that gave them a keener vision, but also a deeper feeling of shock and pain, than others had, and this forced them to speak out. Did they have a mission from God, or had they taken God's work into their own hands?

There can be no denying that the Church was sick. The reforms "in head and members" that had so long been neglected and so often deferred were now about to become a reality. The one Christian Church was to be restored and renewed—there

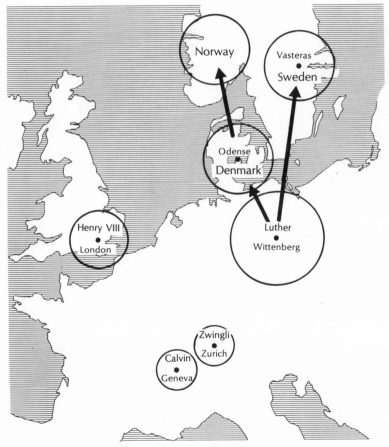

Centers of the Reformation

was, initially, no intention of splitting the Church or founding another Church in opposition to the old one. As late as 1519 Martin Luther was saying, "I never liked the idea of dividing the Church, and I never will."

In the so-called "Reformation of the Princes" there were, along with strictly religious motives, some altogether down-to-earth considerations of political power that lawmakers readily translated into the permanent legal structures of a regional or national church.

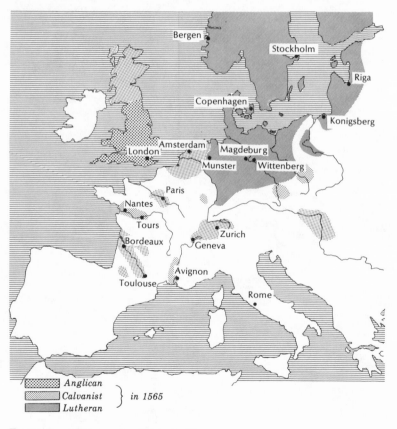

Protestant Denominations in Europe

In discussing the downfall of Catholicism in Scandinavia, the Protestant church historian Karl Heussi trenchantly remarks: "This reform arose, not from the religious needs of the people, but from the political needs of the princes who imposed their restructuring of the Church on the people." Religion was clearly not the issue when the Church of England broke away from Rome over Henry VIII's marital difficulties.

Wittenberg and Geneva—Centers of the Reformation

Just as Martin Luther (1483–1546) put Wittenberg on the map of church and world history, so John Calvin (1509–1564) brought fame to Geneva. The path that transformed Luther from an Augustinian monk into a denominational founder was a long one and paved with many spiritual crises, even though his monastic life and his family life was played out in the same house, the "Black Cloister" of the Hermits of St. Augustine in Wittenberg. Luther's decisive step toward his future as a Reformer (the celebrated "tower experience") came after an evolutionary process of advance-and-retreat. Then on October 31, 1517, when his distress over the Church led him to publish his ninety-five theses, he set off an alarm that was heard far and wide.

Martin Luther "wrestled mightily before God and, as he did, worked his way out of the Church without meaning to," says Joseph Lortz. "Luther's psychic development into a reformer was, at its crucial points, the overthrowing of a Catholicism that was in reality not Catholic. . . . Had it not been for those distortions the schism would never have come about, and had it not been for the hostility and bitterness they engendered the distance separating Catholics and Lutherans would never have become so broad and so permanent."

Over the years Luther's theology and his attachment to the Church underwent a radical change, as a comparison of two texts will clearly show. In May, 1518 Luther wrote to the Medici Pope, Leo X, "I fall at Your Holiness' feet and yield myself up to you with all that I have and am. Let your verdict be life or death; accept me or reject me, approve or condemn, as you please: I shall acknowledge your voice as the voice of Christ that rules and speaks out in you." But in his later years Luther's polemics took on an altogether different tone. In his last great controversial treatise, "Against the Papacy in Rome, Founded by the Devil" (published on March 25, 1545), he wished the following on the Pope and those who would participate in the upcoming Council of Trent (1545–1563): "They should take the Pope, the cardinals, and all the rabble serving His Idolatry and Papal Holiness and rip their tongues right out of their mouths, as blasphemers against God, and then hang them one after the other on the gallows."

Luther saw himself as a pioneer of the word of God and of a Church that would be renewed in the spirit of the Gospel. "He [Christ] must increase, but I must decrease" (Jn 3:30). As a figure in Church history Luther is and will remain subject to the critical judgment of historians. In any event his last words, found on his writing desk after his death (on February 18, 1546 in Eisleben), still move us: "We are beggars. That is true." History proves that the protests and assaults of the Reformers damaged the Roman Church, but they also did it a lot of good.

John Calvin (1509–1564) was entirely different from Luther, both as a man and as a theologian. Because of his conviction that the spirit of God is free, Luther had a strong antipathy to the idea of institutionalizing grace, of pronouncing on its availability. By contrast Calvin was a great legal mind, a pragmatist, the organizer of the *Cité de Dieu,* the City of God in Geneva. Calvin defended the necessity of visible organizations, of regulations and church discipline. The most un-Calvinistic statement imaginable would be that religion is a private affair.

Calvin, a man consumed by zeal for the honor of God and his Kingdom, saw the world as the theater of God's glory. The motto and battle cry of his life, *"Soli Deo gloria"* (To God alone be the glory), bears a disconcerting similarity to Ignatius Loyola's *"Ad majorem Dei gloriam"* (To the greater glory of God). Calvin gave definitive shape to his theological position in the final edition (1559) of his *Institutio christianae religionis* (Instruction in the Christian Religion). The key points were contemplation and honoring of God, God's unlimited sovereignty and freedom. Calvin proposed a radical doctrine of predestination: man has no influence on either his election or rejection by God's inscrutable decree. As expounded by Calvin's friend and follower Theodore Beza (1519–1605), Calvin's teaching on predestination became the core of orthodox Calvinism.

Calvin may have agreed with Luther on many theological and ecclesiastical issues, but an unbridgeable gap opened up over the Eucharist. Calvin firmly resisted Luther's notion of the "real presence," which, he said, "pulls Christ into the bread." In Calvin's opinion the eucharistic forms of bread and wine were no more than the seal, the pledge, the sign of God's saving action.

The theology and church government that Calvin developed and put into practice spread out from Geneva to almost all of Europe. In the Netherlands, France, England, and Scotland they would go on to other—and sometimes quite dramatic—historical destinies.

Courageous Fidelity to the Church

The Church in the fifteenth and sixteenth centuries was not simply a collection of corrupt, money-hungry Christians obsessed by indulgences and adhering to a disastrously fragmented faith. Two examples will have to serve for the many brave men and women who bore faithful witness to the Church: Charitas Pirckheimer, the abbess of the convent of St. Clare in Nuremberg (1467–1532) and Thomas More, the lord chancellor of England (1478–1535).

In her *Memoirs* Charitas Pirckheimer reports about the year 1524: "Owing to the new doctrine of Lutheranism a great many things have changed, and in many places the state of the clergy has almost gone to ruin; for the preaching is of Christian freedom. The laws of the Church, they say, and the vows of religious no longer hold, and no one is bound to keep them. Thus it happens that many nuns and monks, making use of this freedom, have run off from the monasteries and cast their habit off, and some have married and done as they pleased."

The city council of Nuremberg, which had gone over to Lutheranism, wanted to provide the sisters of St. Clare's convent with preachers of the new doctrine. Abbess Pirckheimer informed them in no uncertain terms: "To send lay priests to me and my convent would be an outrageous insult. We would prefer—and it would serve the council better—if you were to send a hangman into our convent to cut our heads off. . . . We wish to stand by the text of the holy Gospel, and neither death nor life shall keep us from it." On March 19, 1525 two of the councilmen ordered the convent to be closed and the sisters to convert to the new teaching. Once more the abbess gave a clear answer: "In what concerns our souls we can follow no one but our own conscience. The mind and conscience must be free, for God, the Lord of all, himself wants the conscience to be free, and not to constrain us. . . . With the help of the living God, whether in life or in death we wish never to break away from our mother, holy Christendom, nor from the things that we have promised to God."

In her last letter the abbess speaks about the painful situation of having to live and die in the convent without priests and the sacraments: "We are such poor, wretched children, sitting in darkness and the shadow of death, deprived of all the holy sacraments, of the Mass, of divine worship, and of guidance from our superiors, which is especially painful in these anxious times, with so many wild and brutal goings-on." The letter must have won the begrudging respect of the Nuremberg city council, because they granted Abbess Pirckheimer, that bold champion of freedom of religion and conscience, and her loyal sisters the right to remain in the convent of St. Clare till the end of their lives.

Placed in an altogether different position, on a lonely political eminence amid explosive problems, Thomas More showed unflinching fidelity to his mother Church. Even the Marxist writer Karl Kautsky couldn't conceal his high regard for More's tremendous integrity when he said, "One can't deal with More without learning to love him." Thomas More, who welcomed men like Erasmus of Rotterdam and Hans Holbein into his house, was not just an erudite humanist, but an excellent jurist, called by Henry VIII to be his lord chancellor. More put his career and his whole life on the line when he felt that he could not "go along," and he refused to be exploited as the king's tool against his conscience and his God.

When Henry let him in on his plans for divorce and remarriage, More loyally took the part of the king, whom he wished to help. But in time he realized that he could not. In 1534 More was tried on charges of high treason. After almost a year and a half in the Tower of London he was beheaded on July 6, 1535. His last words, testifying to both his fidelity to the Church and his solicitude for the king, were, "God grant that my death may profit the king. I die as the king's good servant, but as God's servant first."

Forces for Reform within the Church

Just when the renewal of the Church was being proclaimed in Germany and Switzerland, and when many people no longer believed that the Catholic Church, now grown old, inflexible, and discredited, could renew itself religiously, that renewal actually began. This was not, in fact, a response to the demands and activities of the Reformers. But reform there was, especially in Spain, a quiet, successful wave of reform that spread across Spanish territory.

Ever since the end of the fifteenth century Spain had been enjoying a national euphoria. In 1492, the year Columbus discovered the New World, the country finally managed to capture Granada and end Moorish rule. A "Spanish century" (1480–1580) had dawned, profoundly affecting the arts, philosophy, theology, and piety. To some Catholics Spain seemed to be a land specially chosen by divine Providence. And along with patriotic enthusiasm forces of religious renewal were awake and stirring.

It must be considered fortunate that these reforming energies were able, in the beginning, to go largely unnoticed and acquire greater purity, strength, and depth, for the most part behind monastery walls. The silence and mystical prayer of the cloister—one thinks of Teresa of Avila (d. 1582) or John of the Cross (d. 1591)—were the source of many later reforms in the

Church of Rome. With their bold vision of a renewed, devout, and credible Church the Spanish mystics passed on a contagious passion for religion to Western Christendom. New orders were founded, dedicated to pastoral care, nursing the sick, and the education and formation of youth, as well as to missionary work in the newly discovered regions of the earth.

It was a happy moment in Church history when, after Pope and emperor had quarreled all too long over the time and place it should be held, the Council of Trent was finally convened for its first session on December 13, 1545. Despite everything that had happened, the Church still had the strength and courage to enter on its future path with a convincing sense of identity and a respectful, creative continuity (following Scripture and tradition) with the past. The Council of Trent (1545–1563) has remained a significant directive force all the way into the twentieth century. The Protestant church historian Adolf von Harnack points out that the *Decree on Justification,* proclaimed in the sixth session on January 13, 1547, was a masterful achievement, but came too late: "Had the Tridentine decree on justification been in place before, Luther's appearance would probably have been unnecessary." On the reform of the Catholic Church Peter Meinhold writes: "In a 'Catholic Reformation' the Catholic Church made up for lost time and met all the demands that Protestants had been making of it."

Renewal—and Division Anyway

If we are to understand what really happened in the life and work of Luther, Zwingli, or Calvin, and to avoid blaming the Reformers for later developments, the following point must be kept in mind: Martin Luther, like other Reformers, lived and worked, prayed, struggled and suffered in a "pre-denominational" era. "Just as Luther himself came out of the Roman Catholic world and in many ways remained in it till his death, so his writings were always aimed exclusively at his Roman Catholic fellow Christians and contemporaries," says historian Karl Steck. "For the split of Western Christendom into at least two major groups, which we take for granted, was indeed in the offing, but it became a permanent reality only after Luther's death. . . . At all events Luther wrote only for Catholics, and it was Catholics who felt attracted or repelled by his findings, by his new understanding of Christianity. . . . Luther never envisaged the Christianity split up into 'confessions' that we know today (and view as perfectly natural), and he would scarcely have approved it."

Nonetheless, on the subject of the origin of conflicting confessions it must be said that Martin Luther passively permitted rather than actively shaped the development of the Reformation, insofar as it led to new church systems and political sovereignty over the Church on the part of princes or rulers. The split in the Church was due less to theologians than to political leaders. Martin Luther must have had some notion of this, because his misgivings over it drove him to say, during some "table talk" from the year 1544: "We theologians have no worse enemies than the politicians. . . . That is why we condemn all politicians, even the godly ones, for they don't know what the Church is." Only in 1555 did the Peace of Augsburg bring a divided Church and the beginning of the denominational era.

Key Dates in Church History

1439	Decree of Union passed by the Council of Ferrara-Florence
1498	Conviction and burning of Savonarola in Florence
1500	Christian missions reach out to Mexico, South America, Africa, India, China, and Japan
1517	Publication of the ninety-five theses by Martin Luther
1530	Imperial Diet at Augsburg (Confessio Augustana)
1545–63	Council of Trent
1555	Peace of Augsburg ("Cuius regio, eius et religio")

Chronology

CHURCH HISTORY	SECULAR HISTORY
1414–18 Council of Constance **1415** Jan Hus (1370–1415) burned at the stake **1417–31** Pope Nicholas V **1429** Joan of Arc condemned as a heretic and burned in Reims **1431–47** Pope Eugene IV **1431–47** (17th Ecumenical) Council of Basel (1431– 33)—Ferrara (1438)— Florence (1439–42)—Rome (1442–47)	**1415** Battle of Agincourt— French defeated by Henry V of England
1447–55 Pope Nicholas V	**1440–93** Emperor Frederick II of Germany **ca. 1450** Discovery of the art of printing by Johan Gutenberg (d. 1468) **1453** Capture of Constantinople by Sultan Mohammed II (1451–81)—end of the Eastern Roman Empire
1455–58 Pope Callistus III **1458–64** Pope Pius II **1464–71** Pope Paul II	
1471–84 Pope Sixtus IV	**1465–1536** Erasmus of Rotterdam **1469–1527** Niccolò Machiavelli **1471–1528** Albrecht Dürer **1473–1543** Nicholas Copernicus
1480 Martin Luther born in Eisleben (Saxony) **1484–92** Pope Innocent VIII	

CHURCH HISTORY	SECULAR HISTORY
1484–1531 Huldreich Zwingli **1486–1543** Johannes Eck **1487** Publication of the *Malleus Maleficarum* (persecution of witches) **1491–1556** Ignatius Loyola **1492–1503** Pope Alexander VI **1498** Conviction and burning at the stake of Savonarola in Florence **1503** Pope Pius III **1503–13** Pope Julius II **1509–64** John Calvin **1512–17** (5th) Lateran Council in Rome (closed on March 16, 1517)	**1492** Conquest of Granada—the end of Moorish rule in Spain **1492** Discovery of the "New World" by Christopher Columbus (1451–1506) **1494** Treaty of Tordesillas; establishment of the line of demarcation between the Spanish and Portuguese colonies and missions by Pope Alexander VI **1497–1560** Philipp Melanchthon **1502** Founding of the University of Wittenberg **1509–47** Henry VIII, king of England **1512** Protest lodged by the Dominican Bartolome de las Casas (1472–1566) before Emperor Charles V on account of the exploitation of the Indians by the Spanish conquistadors

CHURCH HISTORY	SECULAR HISTORY
1513–21 Pope Leo X	
	1515–47 Francis I, king of France
1517 Publication of the ninety-five theses by Martin Luther	
	1519–22 First circumnavigation of the world by Ferdinand Magellan
1519 Disputation at Leipzig between Luther and Eck	
	1519–56 Emperor Charles V
1521 Martin Luther at the Diet of Worms—Edict of Worms	**1521** Cortez captures Mexico City
1521–97 Peter Canisius	
1522–23 Pope Hadrian VI	
1523–34 Pope Clement VII	
	1524–25 Peasants' War in Germany
1527 Imperial Diet at Västeras: introduction of the Reformation into Sweden	**1527** The sack of Rome
1529 Marburg Colloquium between Luther and Zwingli	**1529** Siege of Vienna by the Turks under Suleiman II (1520–1566)
1530 Imperial Diet at Augsburg—Augsburg Confession	
	1531 Schmalkaldic League (alliance of Protestant members of the Diet against the religious policy of Emperor Charles V)
1534 Henry VIII declared supreme head of the Church of England	**1534** Jacques Cartier explores the St. Lawrence River
1534–49 Pope Paul III	
1535 Execution of Thomas More in London	

CHURCH HISTORY	SECULAR HISTORY
1536 Introduction of the Reformation into Denmark and Norway	
1541 Introduction of the Reformation into Scotland by John Knox (1513–72)	
1545–63 Council of Trent: three interrupted sessions, 1545–49, 1551–52, 1562–63	
New Orders:	
Theatines (1524)	
Capuchins (1528)	
Jesuits (1534)	
Ursulines (1535)	
Hospitalers (1550)	
Oratorians (1564)	
1546 Death of Martin Luther	
1550–55 Pope Julius III	
1552 Death of the Jesuit missionary Francis Xavier (1506–52) on the island of Sancian near Canton, China	
1555 Peace of Augsburg	
1555 Pope Marcellus II	
1555–59 Pope Paul IV	
	1556 Abdication of Emperor Charles V (d. 1558)
	1558–1603 Elizabeth I, queen of England
1559–65 Pope Pius IV	
	1562–98 Huguenot* Wars in France
1556–72 Pope Pius V	
	1565 Spanish land at St. Augustine, Florida
1566 Roman Catechism published	

CHURCH HISTORY	SECULAR HISTORY
1569 Christian missions reach the Philippines **1570** Roman Missal published	
	1571 (October 7) Destruction of the Turkish fleet in the Gulf of Lepanto **1572** (Aug. 24) St. Bartholomew's Day Massacre
1582 Death of the Spanish Carmelite Teresa of Avila (born 1515) **1583** Christian Missions reach China—Matteo Ricci (1552–1610) **1587** Persecution of Christians in Nagasaki	**1586** First English Settlement in Virginia
	1588 Defeat of the Spanish Armada **1598** Edict of Nantes (freedom of religion for Huguenots)

7

A Superfluous Church?
The Seventeenth and Eighteenth
Centuries

The Reformers' critique of the Church raised many questions
and challenges, to which the Council of Trent gave clarifying
answers and guiding impulses for theology and pastoral work.
But the basic issue of the Church which stirred up such controversy and scandal—and not only among the Reformers—was
not dealt with. The lack of a clear doctrinal statement on the
Church and the unsettled issue of conciliarism (whether a council had supreme authority over the Pope) gave rise in the next
two centuries to theological uncertainties that reverberated
into the 1800's and even the 1900's.

There was no theological center, no point of orientation for
the spiritual trends of the Enlightenment, so they underwent
an undreamed-of fragmentation. Not only did they overlap one
another but they often veered into extremism.

Complexity and Polarization in the Enlightenment

Gottlieb Söhngen notes that the Enlightenment period is
as relevant today as ever: "Since the Enlightenment the various intellectual movements of the day, from romanticism to
the chaotic contemporary scene, have been secretly nourished
by the key decisions made during the Enlightenment—more so
than is generally admitted. . . . And Christian theology in our

time still faces the burdensome task of coming to more comprehensive and penetrating terms with the great questions that the Enlightenment first raised in so radical a fashion."

The intellectual, religious, and artistic palette of the Enlightenment is an astonishingly broad and colorful one. Its many shades span a number of spectrums, from rationalism to mysticism, from empiricism to baroque and rococo art. In music the age was enriched by Händel (d. 1759), Mozart (d. 1791), and Haydn (d. 1809). While rationalism was making inroads into theology and preaching, there was also an upsurge in religious life, with the practice of eucharistic adoration, devotions to the Child Jesus, the Sacred Heart, and Mary, the nuptial mysticism practiced in many covents, the Jesuit theater, plays for Christmas, the Passion, and Easter, and the popular hymns that served as a catechetical accompaniment to the liturgical year.

After the papacy had won new respect through the Council of Trent and the slowly implemented process of pastoral reform, an alliance developed between the Vatican and the "little people." The progressive ideas of reformed Catholicism, with its anti-papal mentality, got nowhere with simple believers who clung to the veneration of the saints, to splendid Corpus Christi processions and pilgrimages, and to exposition of the Blessed Sacrament on altars ablaze with candles. Such fidelity to the Church was marked, on the one hand, by concern for tradition and, on the other, by feast days and ceremonies in which the pious heart could thrill and catch a glimpse of heaven while still on earth.

The Church—A Foreign Body

This was an age when European Christendom was racked by wars of religion that went on for decades, offering the scandalous spectacle, painted in blood and tears, of religious division and naked political ambition, an age when the call for tolerance and the human rights of freedom of conscience could no longer be suppressed. And so the Church, which presented itself to humanity with its dogmas and stern moral code, inevitably ran up against the knife of public criticism.

Alongside the radical skeptics and atheists there were a good number of thinkers who argued for the freedom and breadth of "natural religion," as opposed to the Church's dogmatic faith. The German poet Gotthold Ephraim Lessing gave powerful and appealing expression to the idea that true religion could never be found and so all religions ought to be treated with equal respect.

Although the king of Prussia, Frederick the Great, was the supreme head of the Prussian church, he had a motto: "In my state everyone can find salvation in his own fashion." Anyone who made a claim, as did the Catholic Church, to some absolute status (the "one true Church") was dismissed in advance as suspect, intolerant, outmoded. To allow the crucial decisions of one's life to be made by an outside authority was regarded as a sign of medieval obscurantism and ignoble dependence upon a Church that had not recognized or refused to recognize and accept the signs of a new time and a new freedom.

In an essay called "What Is Enlightenment?" published in 1784, Immanuel Kant (1724–1804) summed up the Enlightenment spirit of longing and daring for many people who felt the way he did: "Enlightenment is man's release from his self-incurred tutelage. Tutelage is man's inability to make use of his understanding without direction from another. Self-incurred is this tutelage when its cause lies not in lack of reason but in lack of resolution and courage to use it without direction from another. *Sapere aude!* 'Have courage to use your own reason!'—that is the motto of enlightenment."

Among intellectuals (or those who thought of themselves as intellectuals) the Church had fallen into discredit because it had been misused (or let itself be misused) to support and defend an aristocratic church. The "reformed Catholicism" of the enlightened absolute rulers was all too often interested not in theological reform but rather in the confiscation of Church property. The Church was downgraded to an educational institute operating "by the grace of the prince." The absolutist rulers acknowledged its political and pedagogical task—of forming and motivating loyal subjects, conscientious taxpayers, and brave soldiers ready to die for "throne and altar." The Church had to see that "law and order" were maintained; it had to prevent revolution.

Emperor Joseph II, who as the "arch-sacristan" of the Holy Roman Empire prescribed how long sermons should be and how many candles were to be lit, had his advisor draw up a statement of the Catholic Church's role as follows: "The Church is to be a moral police department that must serve the goals of the state until such time as the enlightenment of the people permits the state's police force to take over the job."

For a regime that thought of itself in this way the Church was still tolerated, but the end of its useful life was projected into the foreseeable future. The Church was superfluous. But because the Church let itself be used and misused to insure princely absolutism, and because most of the Church's high officials in that era came from the ranks of the nobility (the aristocratic Church), the day could virtually be predicted when a massive protest would have to swell up against both throne and altar: their unholy alliance led into the abyss of a common catastrophe.

A Church that was content to be assigned a pedagogical-didactic-moralizing function by a gracious prince and to look after the preservation of the monarchy, of the aristocratic Church with its lucrative benefices, and of the social status quo had forgotten that, as Jesus said, it was in this world but not of it.

The Case of Galileo and Its Consequences

The case of Galileo provides a classic example of the problems the Church had with the manifold developments of modern philosophy, but above all with science. In February 1616 the Roman Inquisition condemned the basic theses of the celebrated work *De revolutionibus orbium coelestium* by Nicholas Copernicus (1473–1543), namely that the sun is the center of the planetary system and that the earth revolves about its axis and the sun. In 1633 the Church felt that it had to make an example of Galileo Galilei (1564–1642), and so the court of the Inquisition in Rome condemned his *Dialogue on the Two Great Systems of the World,* which had been published in 1623.

In this new vision of the universe the Church thought it saw a massive attack on the inerrancy of Holy Scripture. The heliocentrism that Copernicus advocated and Galileo defended threatened people's belief in creation and biblical exegesis in general. The geocentric world picture of the Greek astronomer Ptolemy was considered an inseparable part of the Bible and a matter of faith. Denying the "scriptural" world picture was equivalent to unbelief, and so on June 22, 1633 Galileo and his teaching were convicted of error.

Some have tried to excuse this deplorable miscarriage of justice by arguing that in the course of publishing his work and standing trial before the Inquisition Galileo played a rather peculiar, underhanded role and violated his scientific conscience by pretending that he didn't really accept the condemned teachings of Copernicus. But this argument will not do. The fact remains that the Inquisition rendered a judgment which shows how stubbornly the Church holds on to outmoded ideas and how skeptically it often regards the expansion of intellectual horizons. "The whole affair followed the law of intellectual development that every new finding has to win a place for itself and overcome the initial resistance of prevailing points of view, thereby demonstrating its power and coherence and gradually compelling assent from thinking people everywhere," said Albert Ehrhard.

The case of Galileo had incalculable consequences for the Church. Historian Friedrich Dessauer does not hesitate to rank it with the Eastern Schism and the Protestant Reformation as the third great catastrophe in Church history: "The first two were grave enough, but for all that those who left the Church have not vanished: they have remained Christians, and while the divisions have not healed, neither have they deepened. But the third is a positive chasm that runs through every nation in the world."

The Chinese Rite Controversy

With the discovery of the New World an upsurge of missionary activity began in Spanish and Portuguese colonial territories, which had been clearly separated by Pope Alexander VI's line of demarcation in 1493. In this process of evangelization political and missionary interests occasionally became entangled in some strange and scandalous ways. Some missionaries appeared with a sword in one hand and the Gospels in the other.

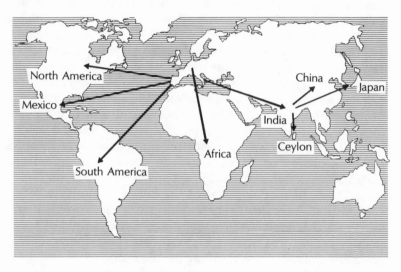

Missions at the Dawn of the Modern Age

In order to protect the native populations from the depredations of the "Christian" conquerors, the Jesuits, beginning around 1610, built settlements, called reductions, for the Christian Indians in Paraguay. Eventually they managed to set up an "Indian state." The Jesuit reductions in Paraguay may have had many shortcomings, but it should be noted that they were more or less a necessity, and a legal kind of self-help against the danger of exploitation and extermination that threatened from all sides.

In the Far East, meanwhile, a quite different missionary field was opening up. Back in the late Middle Ages (from about 1250 on) Franciscans and Dominicans had journeyed to India and China by land and (whether from the Near East or India) by water. One of the first evangelists to arrive in the Far East via the Cape of Good Hope was the Jesuit Francis Xavier (1506–1552). A springtime for missionary work and the Christian faith, with justifiably great future hopes, now came to India, China, and Japan.

One fundamental question, over which Franciscans, Dominicans, and Jesuits could not agree, overshadowed the whole mission to the Far East: Should Christianity be transmitted in the "packaging" of Western culture and its conceptual language, or does every culture and society have the right to its own peculiar embodiment of the Christian message? The Jesuits were for the greatest possible accommodation, and not only in the clothing and external demeanor of their missionaries. They proposed to move beyond that to making a serious study of indigenous cultures and adapting Christianity to them, making a fresh translation of the Christian message into the expressive modes of India, China, and Japan. They argued that baptized Chinese should be allowed to retain the traditional custom of venerating their ancestors, including Confucius.

The champions of this broad-minded and flexible accommodation were the Jesuit missionaries Roberto de Nobili (1577–1656) in India, Matteo Ricci (1552–1610) in Japan, and Johann Adam Schall (1591–1666) in China. Back in Europe church authorities feared that the substance of Christianity would be dismantled and betrayed by too much accommodation, and among the missionaries themselves working in the Far East there were open rivalries and charges of heresy.

The Chinese rite controversy lasted almost one hundred years, until Pope Benedict XIV (1740–58) put an end to it with the Apostolic Constitution *Ex quo singulari* (July 11, 1742). Terrible damage was done to the Far East missions, especially in China, by the struggles among the different missionary orders and by the colonialism of the European "protecting powers." The hopeful springtime of the Far Eastern mission was struck by a calamitous frost. From the eighteenth century onward the mission stagnated, lost its credibility, and underwent persecution.

The great dialogue of Christianity with the cultures and social systems of the Far East had failed. The missionary orders, the theology that inspired them, and the Church's hierarchy were not yet mature enough to put into practice a bold but necessary incarnation of the Christian message in foreign cultures through a dynamic process of fusion. In so doing they would have expanded the horizon of the Western Church to that of a truly catholic world Church, in which every nation, with its own language and culture, would be fully naturalized. The unity of the Church, its leaders still thought, depended on keeping the same forms and formulas used in Europe. It took a long series of experiences before the Church came to learn (remembering the original Christian awakening of Pentecost) that unity lies in multiplicity, so as to open the way to legitimate pluralism in a single body.

Weakness of the Papacy

At the high tide of princely absolutism, when monarchs who were supported by national aristocratic churches favorable to their interests and bound to them by all sorts of kinships were concentrating more and more power in their hands, it was inevitable that they would clash with the Pope, who was himself a political sovereign. Other important factors that led to this clash were the new trends of modern philosophy and the fascination with the natural sciences which led to vehement assaults on the supernatural, on any sort of belief in revelation, and finally to attacks on a reactionary Church. In this period the prestige and influence of the papacy reached a lower point than it had known for centuries, causing its enemies to believe that its downfall had come. The decline of the papacy was not the fault of the men who occupied the chair of St. Peter in the eighteenth century—their personal worthiness was unquestionable. Instead it was the result of radical changes in the political and intellectual situation.

Evidence of how much political pressure was being applied to the Vatican (and by the "good Catholic" rulers of Portugal, France, Spain, and Naples) can be found in the suppression of the Jesuits, decreed by Pope Clement XIV on July 21, 1773. The Jesuits may have been guilty of imprudence, of engaging in power politics under the cover of religion, and of running up unsecured liabilities on debts (as in the case of Fr. Antoine Lavalette). But there were some strange political and theological bedfellows among their enemies (supporters of Gallicanism* and Jansenism,* and competing religious orders), and they organized against the Jesuits, accompanied by a massive propaganda campaign. However varied their motivation, they all agreed on one goal: to remove the Jesuit order once and forever from the stage of Church and world history. In striking out at the Jesuits they were simply attacking a champion of the papacy. And the papacy was meeting opposition not just from the absolutist princes but from quite a few Catholic theologians. Apart from conciliarism, which fought for the supremacy of a Church council over the Pope, there were strong national Church forces that increasingly undermined the authority of the Vatican.

In 1782 when Pius VI (1775–99) attempted to intervene with Emperor Joseph II (1765–90) in Vienna against further restrictions on the Catholic Church, he was received with fitting civility, but dismissed just as politely with empty hands. Ultimately he died in France as a prisoner. His successor Pius VII (1800–23) stood by helplessly in the Cathedral of Notre Dame on December 2, 1804 as Napoleon placed the imperial crown on his own head, laying claim to the throne of Charlemagne. A short time later the Pope was led prisoner to Fontainebleau.

From Innocent III (1198–1216) and Boniface VIII (1294–1303) all the way to Pius VI and VII the Popes had traveled a long road, one marked by proud imperialistic pretensions and by countless humiliations. An era had apparently dawned in which the Church could continue to exist only in the private chapels of individual Christians.

With the storming of the Bastille on July 14, 1789, the beginning of the French Revolution, we see the grandiloquently titled "Age of Constantine" starting to come to a close, though in drawn-out stages. The French Revolution inaugurated a new frame of reference for many aspects of life, and not just in Europe. The Church was not spared by these transformations. Was the sun now setting on the history of the Church, as it declined into powerlessness? Or would there be a dawn of new hopes, of new, unprecedented challenges from the secularized world and of unique chances for dialogue?

Key Dates in Church History

1622	Establishment of the Congregation for the Propagation of the Faith
1633	Condemnation of Galileo by the Court of the Inquisition in Rome
1742	Chinese rite controversy ended by Pope Benedict XIV
1773	Suppression of the Jesuits by Pope Clement XIV
1789	Storming of the Bastille in Paris, the start of the French Revolution

Chronology

CHURCH HISTORY	SECULAR HISTORY
	1600 Giordano Bruno burned as a heretic in Rome
1608 Missionary work in India by Roberto de Nobili **1609** Establishment of the Jesuit reductions in Paraguay **1615** Mission to China	
	1618–1648 Thirty Years War **1620** Emigration of the Pilgrim fathers to America on the Mayflower
1622 Establishment of the Congregation for the Propagation of the Faith **1623–44** Pope Urban VIII	**1626** New Amsterdam (later New York) founded by the Dutch
1633 Condemnation of Galileo (1564–1642) by the Inquisition	
	1634 Catholic colonists settle in Maryland
New Religious Orders: The Institute of Mary (1609) Lazarists (1625) Sisters of Charity (1639) Trappists (1664) Passionists (1725) Redemptorists (1732)	
	Philosophy: René Descartes (1596–1650) Blaise Pascal (1623–1662) John Locke (1623–1704) Benedict Spinoza (1632–1677) Gottfried Wilhelm Leibnitz (1646–1716) Voltaire (1694–1778)

CHURCH HISTORY	SECULAR HISTORY
	David Hume (1711–1776) Jean Jacques Rousseau (1712–1778) Immanuel Kant (1724–1804)
1639 Roger Williams founds Baptist Church in Providence, R.I.	**1643–1715** King Louis XIV of France, the "Sun King" **1648** (October 24) Peace of Westphalia
1633 Chinese rite controversy between Jesuits, Franciscans, and Dominicans begins **1682** Declaration of the French clergy on the "Freedoms of the Gallican Church"	**1653** Oliver Cromwell becomes Lord Protector of Britain **1673** Jacques Marquette explores the Mississippi River **1679** Junipero Serra founds San Diego mission **1683** Siege of Vienna by the Turks
1685 Revocation of the Edict of Nantes	**1689–1725** Peter the Great, tsar of Russia
1700 Eusebio Kino founds Catholic mission in Tucson	**1717** Foundation of the Grand Lodge of the Freemasons in London **1721** Restructuring of the Russian church by Peter the Great
1731 Moravian church mission to Eskimos in Greenland **1740–58** Pope Benedict XIV	**1740–80** Empress Maria Theresa of Austria **1740–86** King Frederick the Great of Prussia

CHURCH HISTORY	SECULAR HISTORY
1742 End of the Chinese rite controversy	
1763 Johann Nikolaus von Hontheim, suffragan bishop of Trier, using the pseudonym "Justinus Febronius," pubishes *On the Condition of the Church and the Rightful Power of the Bishop of Rome* (Febronianism)	**1754** The French and Indian War begins in North America
	1762–96 Catherine the Great, Empress of Russia
1769–74 Pope Clement XIV	
1773 Suppression of the Jesuits by Pope Clement XIV	
	1774–92 King Louis XVI of France
1775–99 Pope Pius VI	**1775–83** American War of Independence (July 4, 1776)
	1781 Edict of Toleration issued by Emperor Joseph II
	1787 United States Constitution written
	1789 Fall of the Bastille
	1792–1806 Emperor Francis II of Austria

8

The Church of the Future and The Future of the Church: The Nineteenth and Twentieth Centuries

With the French and American Revolutions a new epoch began in practically every area of life, a time of rejection of the past. Alongside that denial went a loud but very discordant chorus affirming the new order. More often than not the concrete shapes of this order, which people struggled so passionately for, could be found only in their dreams.

The reason why the Church was so hard hit by the upheavals and after-effects of the French Revolution is that in its earlier guise of a Church of the aristocracy it had let itself be used and misused to defend a social order that was badly in need of change. It was not surprising, then, that the storm of destruction struck both throne and altar. The foundations of the Age of Constantine were shaken—more than a thousand years of history stamped by the coalition and cooperation between the Church and the Empire. Many Christians, especially bishops and Popes, deluded themselves into believing that this coalition had been permanently established and kept viable by divine Providence.

The Church Deprived of Its Power

The French Revolution and its aftermath brought the curtain down quickly and mercilessly on the aristocratic Church and the protest of reformed Catholicism, with its largely nationalistic mentality. On February 25, 1803 the Deputation of the German Estates meeting in Regensburg decided to secularize the Church, thereby expropriating almost all its property. "Secularization"* was a code name for the forcible transfer of Church property to the state. The reality behind this term was a violation of the law.

Now the Church faced the laborious task of learning an entirely new way of life, one for which the Age of Constantine had not prepared it. The "poor" Church no longer held any appeal for noblemen who before this had often had an hereditary right to positions of leadership in the Church. The lower classes were now providing the pastors. Men from the common people were now being chosen as bishops on account of their religious credibility and concern for the souls entrusted to them.

Secularization created a powerless Church, "poor as a churchmouse," which the state could control all the more easily and reduce to still greater dependency. Owing to the suppression or destruction of almost all monasteries in Europe Catholics lost a group of unique educational centers that had once dotted the land. Monastery schools had once opened the way for many gifted sons of farmers and artisans to intellectual formation, to vocational advancement in the arts and sciences, and to careers as leaders in the Church and society. Now that was no longer possible.

Miscarriage of justice though it was, the painful, externally imposed process of secularization proved on balance to be a healthy unburdening for the Church. Left to its own devices the Church would hardly have mustered the strength and courage to free itself from the many encumbrances of property and wealth that had made people lose confidence in it. After a crippling shock the Church had to go through a bitter period of rethinking that strengthened its credibility and chances of survival. If, in the second half of the nineteenth century it had been as powerful, as rich, and as thoroughly in the pocket of the aristocracy as it was around the middle of the eighteenth century, the Church would have been a helpless target for communist attacks because of its wealth and its record of exploitation.

The Era of Concordats

Throughout the nineteenth century Europe underwent a series of upheavals that mortally wounded the old alliance of Church and state. The new, secular governments were hostile to the interests of the Church. In the United States, of course, a new system was bring tried—total separation of Church and state in which all religious groups were given equal freedom to flourish. Europe, however, was not ready for such an experiment, and the Church continued to be cautious of the very idea of "religious freedom" right up to the Second Vatican Council.

Critics occasionally argue that the European Church lost a unique opportunity by not drawing the obvious conclusions from the grief-laden history of the alliance between the Church and the Empire and striving for a separation of Church and state after the American model. But were the leading figures in the churches and the governments in Europe capable of proceeding to such a radical solution? It seems more likely that members of the hierarchy were still mourning the old order and felt obliged to work to restore it.

In any event the Church had to enter into tediously detailed negotiations with many newly powerful princes in order to guarantee its rights of ownership and the chance for individual Catholics, religious orders, etc., to function and develop normally. This was done through treaties called concordats.* The Church's point of departure and bargaining position were highly unfavorable. And so, rather than have Catholics become second-class citizens or be regarded as enemies of the state (so-called Ultramontanes*), the Church signed a large number of concordats in a short time.

On one hand the concordats weakened the power of the bishops; on the other they strengthened that of the Popes, especially their right to consultation and the final word in appointing bishops. The Catholic charitable work in hospitals and homes for the blind and handicapped, educational efforts in Church kindergartens, and monastery or convent boarding schools, and the abundance of religious associations and educational institutions for children and adults—all this now under the protection of the concordats—served the whole population of a country and not just Catholics. The era of the concordats paved the way for the Church's renewal and increased credibility. But it also motivated and activated Christians in their sense of political and social responsibililty.

Many concordats had a painful history. To be sure, in politically explosive times concordats gave Catholics legal relief and access to the courts. But concordats could be dodged or ignored. Thus in his 1937 encyclical *Mit brennender Sorge* Pope Pius XI issued a loud protest to the whole world over the ways the Hitler regime had evaded, misinterpreted, undermined, and violated the Church-state concordat in Germany.

In the United States the Catholic Church was composed largely of European immigrants, most of them poor, who were fleeing economic and religious strife in the Old World. Because of their low economic status, these immigrants became targets of persecution in a country that was supposed to be a land of tolerance. Opposition to the tide of Catholic immigration took form in the movement known as Nativism* which pitted native-born (mostly Protestant) Americans against newly-arriving Catholics and Jews. Most of the hostility was confined to slanderous exchanges in newspapers and lecture halls, but occasionally it boiled over into full-scale riots.

The Church under Intellectual Siege

From the middle of the nineteenth century on, the Church confronted a new menace to its existence in the shape of a motley coalition of philosophical, scientific, social-revolutionary, and political schools of thought: agnosticism,* atheism, materialism, indifferentism,* liberalism,* communism, Marxism. In addition there was a strong religious and philosophical ferment going on outside the mainstream churches, as the large number of new religious groups, sects, and movements founded in the nineteenth century testifies.

The Church in Europe and America came to think of itself as a beleaguered citadel, which the tidal waves of the modern age were threatening to sweep away. If up to this point the

Church had been open to the world and ready for dialogue, it now increasingly withdrew behind high, safe walls. The Church lapsed into a sort of fortress mentality that paralyzed it and misled it into a series of unhealthy reactions. All too quickly anathemas,* authoritarian condemnations and restrictions came to replace badly needed dialogue and clarifications. Much too hastily Church leaders cast a cloud of suspicion over new concepts in philosophy and theology.

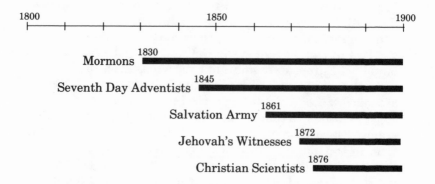

A typical product of this era of perplexity and fear of human rights and democracy was the encyclical *Mirari vos,* issued in 1832 by Pope Gregory XVI. In it the Pope pointed with alarm to "the insane notion that universal freedom of conscience should be proclaimed and fought for. The road to this pestiferous error has been paved by that excessive and extravagant freedom of thought which is spreading far and wide, damaging both the Church and civil society."

Just how vigorously the Church resisted modern philosophical, scientific, and democratic tendencies can be seen in the life of Pope Pius IX (1846–78). He began as a "liberal" and reform-minded Pope, but, largely because of the loss of the Papal States and personal disappointments, he became increasingly skeptical and negative about modernism. While Pope Pius IX loudly proclaimed his readiness to die a martyr in the defense of the Papal States, the Church historian Ignaz von Döllinger took a broader view when he said: "There was a Church and a papacy before the Papal States existed, and Church and papacy will still be there even after the Papal States are lost and gone."

The hierarchical Church and the pastoral Church reacted in sharply different ways to the problems and crises of the period. The hierarchy thought it was obliged to lay down clear theological and pastoral guidelines and to send out a strong call for solidarity and *esprit de corps*. In 1864 Pius IX rejected the most important errors of the nineteenth century in his famous *Syllabus*. Then in 1879 Pope Leo XIII (1878–1903) gave the crucial impetus for Neo-Scholasticism* and Neo-Thomism* by declaring Thomas Aquinas (1225–74) the standard for judging all Catholic philosophy and theology. The Church developed an outlook stressing "safety," and so it demanded uniform theology and preaching, with a strong Scholastic accent.

The reaction of the pastoral Church was altogether different. The crisis in pastoral care and an unbroken tradition of loyalty to the Church combined to foster an unexpected blossoming of religious life. Many new congregations were founded by parish priests in order to get co-workers in the vital areas of pastoral care (kindergartens, hospitals, youth centers, homes for the handicapped). Before World War II a period of a hundred years ended during which, in Germany alone, a new sodality for women was founded every six months.

These new congregations and associations of secular priests were the source of strong and eager volunteers for missionary work all over the world, an influx that, beginning around the middle of the nineteenth century, brought about an extraordinary renaissance of the missions. The Church and its "care of souls" were reborn from the loyalty and faith of the common people and their devout, untiring pastors. Their pastoral zeal was strengthened by the apparitions of Mary at Lourdes (1858), by the exemplary life of Curé of Ars, John Vianney (1786–1859), by the revival of devotion to the Sacred Heart, and certainly too by the encouragement of frequent Communion and earlier Communion for children as urged by Pope Pius X (1903–14).

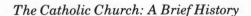

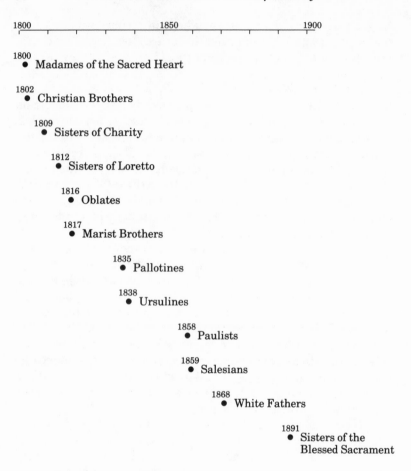

1800   1850   1900

1800
● Madames of the Sacred Heart

1802
● Christian Brothers

1809
● Sisters of Charity

1812
● Sisters of Loretto

1816
● Oblates

1817
● Marist Brothers

1835
● Pallotines

1838
● Ursulines

1858
● Paulists

1859
● Salesians

1868
● White Fathers

1891
● Sisters of the
   Blessed Sacrament

The Church Shifts Toward the Third World

According to one triumphal scenario the Church, over the course of history, would spread to all nations and lands on earth, and at the end of time a well-prepared, Christianized humanity would joyfully await the return of its Lord (1 Cor 11:26). During the twentieth century this idea received an abrupt but beneficial correction. The religious geography of the late twentieth century has been marked, first of all, by a slow but broad pattern of loss of faith and quiet abandonment of the Church. Alongside the two major confessions of Catholicism and Protestantism a "third confession" of the unbaptized and indifferent has been growing up. Friedrich Nietzsche (1844–1900) loudly and scornfully proclaimed the death of God and spoke sarcastically of the churches as God's sepulcres. Among the younger generation there is a large population that seems to have no sense of God, religion, or the Church.

As an instance of the shifting configurations of religious membership, consider the German city of Munich: between 1970 and 1980 Catholics in that city went from 67.4% of the population to 60%, while Protestants went from 22.9% to 19.7%. At the same time people who were neither Catholic nor Protestant nor Jewish (i.e., members of sects or of non-traditional religious or philosophical groups or of the "third confession") increased their share from 9.7% to 20.1%. Any realistic appraisal of the contemporary Church must register the fact that the proportion of Christians to the world's population as a whole has clearly diminished over the last one hundred and fifty years (one of the reasons for this, of course, is the high birth rate among non-Christian African and Asian nations). Around 1850 Christians still made up something like one half the earth's population. By 1950 this share had shrunk to one-third. Even if we assume that in the future Christian missions will be able to operate as freely and successfully as they have in the past, by the year 2000 the proportion of Christians in the world's population (which will then number over six billion) will sink from one-third to one-sixth.

If we break down the Christian group into denominations, it turns out that the Catholic portion of the total population has gone down from 18.4% (1970) to 18% (1976) in a very short time. The Church Universal is on its way back to being a little flock.

The "face" of the Church and its leaders will, however, take on a considerably different look, owing to the now unmistakable shift of Catholic population toward the third world. In 1976 almost 58% of all Catholics lived in the third world. Latin

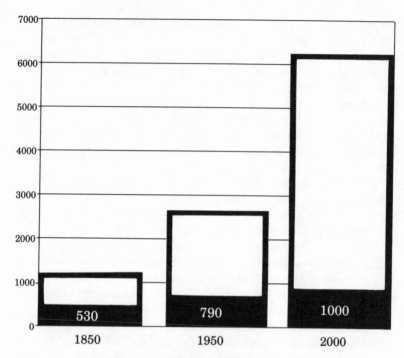

Catholics in Relation to World Population
(numbers in millions)

America seems to be the land where the Church's future hopes are brightest. Within a few years more than half of all Catholics will come from that part of the world.

The Church has already begun to be de-Europeanized, though European and North American Christians have scarcely become aware of it. This in turn will prepare the way for a Church that will be truly universal and Catholic, that will carry out Jesus' charge: "Go therefore and make disciples of all nations" (Mt 28:29). A process of incalculable importance has begun that ought to have profound consequences in the Church's decision-making structure, in the reformulation of dogmas, and in all areas of theology and pastoral care.

How will this departure from the old familiar European

tradition work out? What will be the fate of the Christian message when transformed into brand new cultural dimensions, ways of speaking, and modes of expression? Just as in the first century when the early Christian mission left the narrow limits of Palestine and plunged forward into the great open spaces of the Roman Empire, so at the end of the twentieth century this missionary thrust is extending itself beyond the confines of Europe and North America, so that now for the first time the Church can grow into a worldwide, genuinely Catholic stature.

Ecumenical Unrest

Beginning in the nineteenth century—and still more so in the twentieth—the history of the Church has proved to be a history of the churches—churches that have become nervous about each other, that take each other seriously, talk to each other, pray for each other, share with each other a concern that Jesus' prayer may be realized, "that they also may be one in us, so that the world may believe that thou hast sent me" (Jn 17:21).

In 1824 the Irish Catholic bishop of Kildare-Leighlin, James Warren Doyle, sent a memorandum to the British chancellor of the exchequer that deserves to be remembered as a bold testimony to the spirit of ecumenism.* In it he offers to work for a reunion of the Catholic and Anglican Church. He writes that he personally is ready to give up his office "without payment, without pension, without compensation, without ambition," if this would help unification. He adds: "Out of pride and a false sense of honor we stand aloof from each other on many matters. We lack the love of Christian humility, of our neighbor, and of the truth."

Over the last two hundred years the desire for reuniting separated Christians has refused to be quieted. It has gone beyond the little circles of theological experts and stirred a lively response among Christians everywhere. But the dream of unity has yet to be realized—is it simply because of petty religious politics? Many people have seen their hopes chilled. It is becoming increasingly apparent that an ecumenism which ignores history and truth is of no use to the Church, and, at the same time, that the fragmented state of Christendom is unacceptable for both Christianity and the Church.

A striking landmark in the history of the ecumenical movement was the establishment in 1948 of the World Council of Churches in Amsterdam. In the WCC's Declaration of Principles (Toronto, 1950), which defines its purpose and activities, we read: "The World Council of Churches is not and must never become a superchurch. It is not a superchurch. It is not the world church. It is also not the one true Church that the creeds speak of. . . . By its very existence and activity the Council bears witness to the need for a clear statement on behalf of the unity of Christ's Church. But it remains the right and duty of each church to draw from its ecumenical experience the conclusions to which it feels bound, on the basis of its own peculiar convictions. . . . Membership in the WCC does not imply acceptance of any specific doctrine on the nature of church unity. . . . There is room in the WCC for those churches which recognize other churches as the Church in the full and true sense of the word, and those which do not."

Since then the Second Vatican Council (1962–65) has sent out a series of increasingly strong ecumenical impulses. Even before the Council met, the Secretariat for Christian Unity (with Augustin Cardinal Bea its first president) was founded. Among the important documents of Vatican II concerning ecumenism are the Decree on the Catholic Churches of the East (November 21, 1964), the Decree on Ecumenism (November 20, 1964), and the Declaration on the Relation of the Church to Non-Christian Religions (October 28, 1965). The end of the Council lit a shining beacon when the anathemas from the year 1054, which led to the separation of the Eastern from the Western Church, were solemnly lifted. On December 7, 1965 Pope Paul VI in Rome and Patriarch Athenagoras in Istanbul released identical statements, proclaiming that the schism ought "to be blotted out from the memory of the Church, removed from its midst, and consigned to oblivion."

The history and self-consciousness of present-day Christian churches are marked by ecumenical unrest. Pope John Paul II has said: "Both the will of Christ and the signs of the times impel us to bear joint witness with a growing abundance of truth and love."

The Standpoint and Mandate of the Church

As the twentieth century draws to a close, the religious atmosphere, at least with respect to faith and commitment to the Church, has obviously deteriorated. The breakdowns and losses in the process of handing down the Christian vision, as well as the advances in the secularization and liberalization of thought and life, are impossible to ignore. The first Enlightenment of the seventeenth and eighteenth centuries merely grazed the skin of faith. The second, neo-Enlightenment in the twentieth century has struck at the heart of faith and left it badly wounded.

The personnel problem in the Church—the lack of priests and religious—has manifestly worsened in the second half of this century. Of course, Christ has assured his faithful that "the powers of death shall not prevail against his church" (Mt 16:18). But this in no way means that wherever Christian communities are found today the Christian faith will be preached and the sacraments administered in the next millennium—or even in the next century.

The Church will have to learn to be a "little flock"—with no claim to external power, with none of the chartered rights it enjoyed in the past, if these threaten to encumber and discredit its work. Amidst a much-lamented "eclipse of God" (Martin Buber) we can be thankful that the Church has come to a new vision of itself as the "people of God" and to translate that vision into reality. In Christian communities that have no priests, responsible laypeople make up a Church that can survive and endure.

A Church that sees itself as "God's people" can securely entrust itself to God's guidance. But, according to the Bible, one of the characteristics of God's people (recall the wandering in the wilderness of Sinai) is their susceptibility to betraying the covenant and dancing about the golden calf of homemade idols and utopias.

Like every individual Christian, the Church as a whole

lives in the tension-filled polarity set up by two questions: one directed back at God's revelation, which was transmitted in historical time and space and which reached its supreme and unsurpassable high point in Jesus Christ, and the other directed forward to God's judgment at the end of history. This double inquiry and the continually renewed attempt to deal successfully with both ends of it determine the particular standpoint and mandate of the Church in every stage of its history, today and tomorrow.

Key Dates in Church History

1869–70	First Vatican Council
1948	Establishment and First Plenary Assembly of the World Council of Churches
1962–65	Second Vatican Council

Chronology

CHURCH HISTORY	SECULAR HISTORY
1789 John Carroll of Baltimore becomes first American bishop	**1789** Storming of the Bastille in Paris, outbreak of the French Revolution
1800–23 Pope Pius VII	
1801 Concordat between Napoleon and the Holy See	
	1803 Louisiana Purchase
	1804 Coronation of Napoleon I as emperor in Notre Dame
	1806 Emperor Francis II abdicates the Roman-German imperial crown: end of the Holy Roman Empire
	1812–1815 War between U.S. and Britain
1814 Restoration of the Jesuits	
	1814–15 Congress of Vienna, reorganization of Europe
	1818–83 Karl Marx
1830 *Book of Mormon* published, beginning of the Mormons	
1831–46 Pope Gregory XVI Era of Concordats: France (1801) Italy (1803) Bavaria, Sardinia (1817) Russia, Naples (1818) Netherlands (1827) Switzerland (1828) Spain (1851) Austria (1855)	**1837–1901** Queen Victoria
	1846–47 War between U.S. and Mexico
1814–78 Giovanni M. Mastai-Ferretti (later Pope Pius IX)	
	1847 Famine in Ireland; beginning of large-scale immigration to America

CHURCH HISTORY	SECULAR HISTORY
1844 Anti-Catholic riots in Philadelphia	**1848** *Communist Manifesto* published in London
	1848 Emperor Francis Joseph I of Austria begins rule
1854 (December 8) Promulgation of the dogma of Mary's Immaculate Conception by Pope Pius IX	
1855 Founding of the World Alliance of Young Men's Christian Associations (YMCA) in Paris	
1858 Apparitions of Mary to Bernadette Soubirous at Lourdes	**1860–1864** The American Civil War
1864 Publication of Pius IX's *Syllabus of Errors*	**1864** Geneva Convention (Red Cross)
1869–1870 First Vatican Council: Promulgation of the primacy and infallibility of the Pope	
	1870–71 Franco-Prussian War
1870 End of the Papal States	
1872 Founding of the Jehovah's Witnesses by Charles Russell	
	1874 World Postal Union
1878 Founding of the Salvation Army by Gen. William Booth (d. 1912)	
1878–1903 Pope Leo XIII	**1888** Emperor William II begins reign in Germany
1879 Publication of the encyclical *Aeterni Patris* by Pope Leo XIII (Neo-Scholasticism* and Neo-Thomism*)	
1890 Death of John Henry Cardinal Newman	**1890** Indians massacred at Wounded Knee, S.D.

CHURCH HISTORY	SECULAR HISTORY
1891 Publication of the encyclical *Rerum novarum* by Pope Leo XIII	
	1896 First Olympic Games of modern times celebrated in Athens
	1898 War between U.S. and Spain
1903–14 Pope Pius X	
1907 Publication of the encyclical *Pascendi dominici gregis* (against modernism) by Pope Pius X	**1914–18** First World War
1910 First World Missionary Conference in Edinburgh, forerunner of World Council of Churches	
1914–22 Pope Benedict XV	
	1917 October Revolution in Petrograd, end of the tsarist empire
1917 Apparitions of Our Lady of the Rosary at Fatima, Portugal	
1922–39 Pope Pius XI	**1919** Treaty of Versailles
	1922 Mussolini's march on Rome: fascists seize power in Italy
1925 First World Conference of Churches in Stockholm	
1929 Lateran Treaties between the Vatican and the Mussolini regime in Italy	
1933 (July 20) Signing of the *Reichskonkordat* between the Vatican and Nazi Germany	

CHURCH HISTORY	SECULAR HISTORY
1937 (March 14) Publication of the encyclical *Mit brennender Sorge* (against Nazism) by Pope Pius XI	
1939–58 Pope Pius XII	**1939–1945** Second World War
	1945 Dropping of the first atomic bomb on Hiroshima
	1947 First manuscripts found at Qumran (Dead Sea Scrolls)
1948 Establishment and first Plenary Assembly of the World Council of Churches in Amsterdam	
1950 Promulgation by Pope Pius XII of the dogma of the bodily assumption of Mary into heaven	**1960** John F. Kennedy, a Catholic, elected President of the United States
1958–63 Pope John XXIII	**1961** First man in space, the Soviet astronaut Yuri Gagarin
1963–78 Pope Paul VI	**1969** First men on the moon (astronauts Neil Armstrong and Edwin Aldrin)
1978 Pope John Paul I	
1978 Election of the Polish cardinal Karol Wojtyla as Pope John Paul II	

Glossary

Agnosticism—(from *agnoscere,* Latin for "not to know") Philosophical position (but also a popular attitude) that confines the powers of human understanding to finite reality and rejects any exact or certain knowledge of God and the supernatural. Religious agnosticism can help to remind believers that a God whose existence is proved and comprehended is not the God of the Bible nor the God proclaimed in the Church's creed. God can be known and confessed only as an ungraspable mystery.

Albigensians—Heretics named after the town of Albi in southern France, a center of the Cathars* (beginning in the early twelfth century). They followed the radical, militant line of the Catharist movement and came into sharp conflict with religious and political authorities. After several wars aimed at converting or destroying them (1209–22) their power was broken by the Inquisition in 1330.

Anathema—Formula of rejection by the Church, concluding that a given opinion conflicts with tradition and the faith, as the Church understands them. Only statements are rebuffed; no judgment is passed on the subjective attitude or religious orthodoxy of the person making the statement.

Aristotle—(384–322 B.C.) Greek philosopher, student of Plato (427–347 B.C.), tutor of the future King Alexander the

Great. His philosophical realism is characterized by respect for ordinary experience and by trust in the power of reason, which allows us to move from the visible world to final causes. Aristotle maintains that the human being is at once an individual and an essentially social being. Aristotle's creative achievement and intellectual style, thanks to the mediation of Thomas Aquinas (1225–1274), gave a new impetus to Western philosophy and theology.

Arius—(d. 336) Born in Libya, a priest in Alexandria, he taught that the Son (Jesus Christ) was not eternal like God the Father, but was created by the Father, thus begotten and made as a mediator between God and man. This doctrine (called Arianism) was condemned at the First Council of Nicaea (325), which ruled that the Son is not *like* the Father in nature, as Arius claimed, but of the same essence. Most of the Germanic tribes adopted the Arian form of Christianity and spread it throughout Europe.

Augustine—(Aurelius Augustinus, 354–430) Born in Tagaste (North Africa), he taught rhetoric in Carthage, Rome, and Milan (375–384), was baptized (387) by Bishop Ambrose in Milan, and from 396 was bishop of Hippo (in present-day Algeria). One of the greatest Doctors of the Church, noted for his "theology of the heart." His writings on the theology of history, on the Trinity, and on the meaning and purpose of human life have been and remain important contributions to Western theology, philosophy, psychology, and politics. His main works are *The City of God, On the Trinity,* and the *Confessions.*

Bonaventure—(1221–1274) Original name Giovanni di Fidanza, general of the Franciscans, representative of the older, Augustinian branch of Scholasticism.*

Cathars—(from the Greek *katharoi,* "the pure ones") During the Crusades certain ideas brought back from the East evoked a strong response in the lower Rhineland, in southern France, Italy, and Spain. The center and foundation of the Catharist doctrine is the insurmountable opposition between the soul of the pure individual and the sinful world. The Catharist Council of Toulouse (1167) radicalized the movement's views of the Church, society, and politics (rejection of marriage, property, and war). Of special meaning for the Church at large, given its wealth, was the Catharist stress on "Jesus the poor man" and their call for a poor Church.

Concordat—(from the Latin *concordare,* "agree") A treaty between the Church and a secular state.

Cyprian of Carthage—(200–58) Became bishop of Carthage in 248, clashed with Pope Stephen I (254–57) over the validity of baptism when administered by heretics, died a martyr. Main works: *On the Unity of the Church, On the Apostates, Collected Letters.*

Docetism—Broad philosophical-religious current that (like Neo-Platonism,* Montanism,* and Manichaeism*) started out from the notion that matter was evil. It fought the Church's teaching of the incarnation, arguing instead that Jesus Christ had no material body, only a phantom body, that Christ had only seemed to suffer and die.

Ecumenism—Worldwide efforts to bring together the separated Christian communities into a single faith and Church. Also, a movement among Christians to understand and appreciate their different religious traditions.

Essenes—Jewish sect in the time of Jesus following a rule like that of later religious orders (celibacy, renunciation of private property, a "baptism of repentance"). The group shows certain similarities to the primitive Christian community of Jerusalem. The existence and way of life of the Essenes were confirmed by the sensational finds of manuscripts near the Wadi Qumran (from 1947 on). The most significant personality in the Essene community was surely the "Teacher of Righteousness," who can be described as one of the last prophetic figures of Israel.

Eusebius of Caesarea—(263–339) One of the oldest church historians, called the "Father of Church History." Main work: *Chronicle, Ecclesiastical History, Martyrs of Palestine.*

Gnosis—Philosophical-theological school that tries to resolve the unmastered tension and contradictoriness of existence by arguing that there are two basic principles, one good (God and mind) and the other evil (matter). Building on this dualistic assumption, gnosticism offers a way to salvation in the idea that man can free himself from and atone for the contamination of evil matter through "knowledge" (*gnosis* in Greek). Redemption is to be gained through this knowledge, not through the incarnation and death on the cross of the Son of God made man (cf. Docetism, Manichaeism, Montanism, Neo-Platonism).

Hilary of Poitiers—(d. 367) As bishop of Poitiers, he was a resolute defender of the Church's doctrine of the incarnation. Exiled in the East because of his rejection of Arianism* (356–60), he came to know the writings of the Church Fathers, whose theological arguments he employed masterfully in his battle against Arianism in the West. His works on the Bible prove him to be one of the first important Western exegetes.

Huguenots—The word (probably a nickname, from the German *Eidgenossen,* "confederates") was, from about 1560 onward, used as a general label for French Calvinists. After bloody persecutions King Henry IV granted them freedom of religion and conscience in the Edict of Nantes (1598). King Louis XIV revoked this edict in 1685, so that most of the Calvinists in France were forced to emigrate.

Ignatius of Antioch—(second century) One of the "Apostolic Fathers," along with Clement of Rome (d. 99) and Polycarp of Smyrna (d. 155). In the letters he wrote (107) to the Christian community of Rome he gives pride of place to the church of Rome, which he calls "the head of the alliance of love."

Indifferentism—Total apathy toward religion. Indifferentism often appears in the garb of objectivity and freedom from presuppositions, it can also indicate a lack of courage to make decisions and take stands. Kant called it "the mother of chaos and night."

Irenaeus of Lyon—(ca. 115–202) Born in Asia Minor, where he was a disciple of Polycarp of Smyrna (who had heard John the Apostle), he became bishop of Lyon around 177. In opposition to gnosticism* he emphasized a biblical-Christian valuation of the created world and of the incarnation. Through the incarnation, he writes, the world has become a "holy place," a conviction that resounds in his saying that "The glory of God is a living human being" (*Gloria Dei vivens homo*). Main works: *Against Heresies, Proof of the Apostolic Preaching.*

Jansenism—Religious movement, named after Cornelius Jansen (1585–1638), bishop of Ypres, whose major work, *Augustinus,* was published after his death. Jansenism was widespread in seventeenth and eighteenth century Europe. One of the great centers of Jansenism was the convent of Port Royal near Paris. One of its most famous adherents was the philosopher and mathematician Blaise Pascal (1623–63), who based religious truth on "the reasons of the heart." Chief elements of Jansenism: rejection of philosophy, exclusive authority of Scripture, extreme strictness in morality and religious life (rigorous prerequisites for receiving Holy Communion), stress on the rights of bishops (after the fashion of Gallicanism*). Ac-

cording to the Jansenist understanding of the redemption
Jesus died only for the chosen few, the mass of men are
damned.

Jerome—(340–419) In his day probably the greatest expert on
Latin and Greek, he was given the assignment by Pope Da-
masus I (336–84) of revising the old Latin translation of
the Bible. He retired—in good measure because of the
many conflicts stirred up by his prickly, belligerent character—from Rome to Palestine, where for almost twenty
years he dedicated himself to the task of revising the Latin
Bible. He has been rightly honored with the title "Grand-
father of Biblical Studies." Main works: Vulgate translation of the Bible, biblical commentaries, monastic
biographies, sermons and letters.

Leo I, the Great—As Pope (440–61) championed the authen-
ticity of faith in Christ, as defined by the Council of Chalcedon (451). In a period when the power of the Western
Roman Empire was crumbling he was a brave defender of
Rome in the face of the Huns (see his famous meeting with
Attila in 452) and Genseric, king of the Vandals (455). Leo
significantly increased the authority of the papacy
through his forceful personality and decisive action.

Liberalism—An ambiguous word, used in contradictory ways.
In many instances liberalism arose as a reaction to exces-
sively authoritarian systems and regimentation, whether
on the part of Church or of state. It pointedly defends the
freedom of the individual and the free play of forces in the
political and economic arena. The liberal point of view
must not be equated with independence of mind. True liberal thinking is rooted in respect for the otherness of other
people and in aversion to endangering or destroying the
freedom of one's fellows.

Macedonius—Bishop of Constantinople (deposed in 360), attacked the divinity of the Holy Spirit, whom he viewed as

no more than a creature of the Son. The followers of his doctrine were called *Pneumatomachoi* (Greek for "opponents of the Spirit") and also, after 380, "Macedonians."

Manichaeism—Teaching of the Babylonian Mani (216–277), a syncretistic religion based on Persian, Buddhist, Babylonian-Chaldean, Jewish, and Christian elements. It is animated by the dualistic doctrine of two fundamental principles, supreme Goodness and supreme Evil. Salvation and redemption are achieved by combating evil (Satan, darkness), which is incorporated in the material, physical world. Cf. Gnosis, Docetism, Montanism.

Marcion—Born in Sinope (now northern Turkey), he proposed (ca. 150) an abbreviated, "purified" canon of Holy Scripture, consisting only of the Gospel according to Luke and ten Epistles of Paul (omitting the Pastoral Epistles). Marcion argued for a de-Judaized Church and insisted that the New Testament (the covenant of love) was unalterably opposed to the Old Testament (the covenant of harsh penal justice).

Montanus—(d. 172) Founder of a Christian Gnostic sect that, like Manichaeism, presupposes a dualism of Good (God, Spirit) and Evil (matter). Around 156 he proclaimed the descent of the heavenly Jerusalem (in Phrygia). He advocated hostile ascetic treatment of the body and looked forward to an early beginning of Christ's thousand-year reign on earth. The followers of Montanus, who claimed to enjoy a special enlightenment from the Holy Spirit, called themselves "Pneumatics," in contrast to the members of the main Christian Church ("Psychics") and material-minded individuals ("Hylics," from *hyle*, matter).

Mysticism—The experience of God as an inner vision or as encounter and union, achieved not through rationally comprehensible knowledge but through God's free gift. Christian mysticism is deeply imprinted with the Christian image of God. It is a Trinitarian mysticism empowered by Christ's redemption and granted by the Holy Spirit, the life-giver and Comforter.

Nativism—Movement in nineteenth and early twentieth century America that pitted native-born (i.e., Protestant) citizens against the tide of (largely Catholic) immigrants. Marked by vitriolic attacks, riots. Dwindled after the Civil War, but continued to survive in Ku Klux Klan and similar groups.

Neo-Platonism—Philosophical school of late antiquity (founded by Plotinus, 204–70) that, on the one hand, stimulated Christian thought and life, and, on the other, greatly threatened to distort the evolution of Christianity. (It was hostile to belief in divine creation, the uniqueness of salvation history, the incarnation of the Son of God, positive valuation of this world, the promise of a new heaven and earth at the end of time, the resurrection of the body, etc.)

Neo-Scholasticism—Revival and modernization of medieval Scholastic philosophy and theology, inspired by the encyclical *Aeterni patris* by Pope Leo XIII (August 4, 1879); it promoted both major strands of Scholastic tradition, the Augustinian-Bonaventuran and the Aristotelian-Thomistic approach.

Neo-Thomism—Revival of the philosophy and theology of the Dominican theologian Thomas Aquinas (1225–74). Pope Leo XIII wanted Catholic philosophy and theology to be renewed in the spirit of Thomas so that a coherent system could be brought to bear on the many, largely anti-religious and anti-clerical intellectual trends of the nineteenth century. But to exclude other schools of thought from the realm of Catholic philosophy and theology, and to defend Thomism as the only valid system contradicts Aquinas' characteristic broadmindedness.

Nestorius—(d. around 451) Born in Syria, a priest in Antioch, patriarch of Constantinople, he attacked the notion of the complete, uncurtailed humanity and human personality of Jesus. He saw the divinity and humanity of Jesus as bound together only in a moral sense (as opposed to Jesus' human nature being united to his divine nature in one divine Person). At the Council of Chalcedon (451) the Church defined the doctrine of the "hypostatic union" and the two unmixed natures in Christ. "We confess, not a being divided and dismembered into two persons, but one and the same person, the only begotten Son, the divine Word, the Lord Jesus Christ."

Origen—(185–254) Leader of the catechetical school in Alexandria, and later in Caesarea, he suffered in the persecution of Decius (249–51), and died after the death of Emperor Decius. Main works: *Hexapla* (six-column edition of the Bible, in which alongside the original Hebrew text various Greek translations were placed for comparison), biblical commentaries and homilies, *De principiis* (the oldest manual of Christian dogmatic theology).

Qumran—A monastery (Chirbet Qumran) on the northwest shore of the Dead Sea (ca. ten miles south of Jericho), well known since 1947 on account of the pre-Christian manuscripts discovered in eleven caves, which provided important evidence concerning the text of the Old Testament and the spiritual life of the Essenes.* During the Jewish uprising (132–35 A.D.) Qumran was destroyed by the Romans as a base of support for the Jewish resistance fighter Bar Kochba.

Restoration—Efforts to bring back old conditions, forms and formulas in politics, culture, and religion, generally intended to forestall new ideas and movements.

Scholasticism—A philosophical and theological method developed in the medieval universities and used to explore

the Christian faith, to weigh it carefully in critical, dialec-
tic arguments, and to present it memorably and convinc-
ingly in a systematic body of thought. The same term also
refers to Christian theology as a whole from 800 to 1400.
The basic principle of medieval Scholasticism is the com-
patibility of faith and knowledge and so of the two sources
of knowledge, human reason and divine revelation. Medieval Scholasticism has two main strands, the older Pla-
tonic and Augustinian variety whose spokesmen were the
Franciscans (Bonaventure), and the newer Aristotelian
variety promoted by the Dominicans (Albertus Magnus,
Thomas Aquinas).

Secularization—First used in 1648 by Henri de Longueville,
the word nowadays refers to, among other things, the grad-
ual erosion of religious values in favor of non-religious,
materialistic values.

Tertullian—(ca. 160–220) Born in Carthage, he became a
Christian around 193 in Rome, left the Church sometime
before 205, and became a passionate follower and defender
of the harsh, gloomy doctrine of Montanus.*

Thomas Aquinas—From Aquino (near Naples), disciple of Albertus Magnus (1193–1280), member of the Dominican order. He adopted essential features of Aristotelian
philosophy (respect for the reality of this world, trust in the
power of reason). His thought is characterized by a distinction between reason and revelation (which do not, however, contradict one another), by respect for tradition and
its authorities, and by its goal of systematic synthesis. He
distanced himself from the Augustinian theology of the
past and his own day. According to Aquinas, people gain
knowledge not through the recollection of ideas (as in
Plato), but through sense perception and the analytic
power of reason. He is called the "Prince of Scholasticism."* He has received exemplary recognition from the

Church in both the Neo-Scholasticism* and Neo-Thomism* of the nineteenth and twentieth centuries.

Ultramontanism—(*ultra montes,* Latin, "on the other side of the mountains"). Term of reproach, used especially after the First Vatican Council declared the Pope infallible, implying that Catholics were not autonomous, responsible citizens of their own countries but came to political decisions at the "higher bidding" of the Pope (across the Alps).

Waldensians—Religious movement founded by Peter Valdes (died before 1238) who called for a return to the poverty of Jesus and of the early Church and for intensive reading of Holy Scripture. Later the Waldensians rejected the Church's teaching authority, most of the sacraments (except the baptism of adults, penance, and the Eucharist), veneration of saints and relics, purgatory, and indulgences. These views played a significant role in the Reformation three centuries later.